The Good Old Days Songbook

The GOOD OLD DAYS Songbook

Sixty Songs
from the Golden Age of Music Hall
selected, with an introduction and notes by
Peter Gammond

Foreword by Barney Colehan

BRITISH BROADCASTING CORPORATION
EMI MUSIC PUBLISHING LIMITED

Picture credits:
all songsheet covers on pages 232–247 EMI;
illustrations to Introduction courtesy of Peter Gammond;
photograph page 8 by Ken Heaney.
Cover photograph BBC copyright.

Published by the British Broadcasting Corporation,
35 Marylebone High Street, London W1M 4AA
in association with EMI Music Publishing Limited,
138–140 Charing Cross Road, London WC2H 0LD

ISBN 0 563 17623 7 (BBC)
ISBN 0 86175 143 4 (EMI)
First published 1980

Printed in England by BAS Printers Limited,
Over Wallop, Hampshire

Contents

Alphabetical list of songs

Foreword

The songs to be found in this volume are the songs of the Music Hall, and they recall that era which is often nostalgically called 'the Good Old Days'.

How often have you heard: 'Ladies and Gentlemen, for your delectation and delight we proudly present that personification of pulchritude, that mellifluous model of maidenhood – dare I say "modest"?' The Chairman, Leonard Sachs, bangs the gavel, flourishes his white-gloved hands and in high-flown, alliterative language, wallowing in hyperbole, introduces another visit to old-time music hall at the famous City Varieties Theatre, Leeds. As the gavel bangs, the audience roars its enthusiastic approval and bursts into song.

The first time this happened was at the City Varieties in 1953, when I produced a programme called *The Story of the Music Hall*, which depicted the development of the theatre from its Victorian days to 1953. The Narrator, or 'Spirit of the Theatre' as he was called, was Deryck Guyler. The programme proved so popular that a short series was devised, and the Edwardian music-hall ingredient of the original programme was developed with remarkable success.

At first we had only a few rows of the stalls filled with a dressed audience, but this aspect of the programme seemed to intrigue viewers, and so the demand to be included grew and grew; the waiting list for costume tickets now stands at 24,000.

Gradually, improvements were made to the presentation of the show. The Chairman left the stage and was sited on an illuminated 'run-out', which allowed him to make a flamboyant entrance and, in turn, added another dimension to the presentation of the artists.

Naturally, when the programme made its debut in 1953 it was never envisaged that its popularity would ensure an uninterrupted run of twenty-seven years. What, then, has guaranteed this success? The theatre? The high standard of entertainment? The dressed audience? Undoubtedly all these ingredients, plus – and a big plus – the convivial, community atmosphere created, for audience and viewers alike, by the singable songs and melodious medleys of the 'Good Old Days'.

During those twenty-seven years songs from this album have been presented in *The Good Old Days*, thus depicting the whims and fancies, the joys and sorrows of Edwardian England. Songs are there to be sung; but they are also an index to the life and history of a country. Every aspect of life is reflected in the songs of the music hall: war – *Good-By-Ee*; slang – *Has Anybody Seen my Tiddler*; novelty – *The Tin Gee-Gee*; drink – *I Belong to Glasgow*; flirtation – *When I Take my Morning Promenade*; love – *For me and my Gal*; marriage – *Bill Bailey, Won't you Please Come Home*; parting – *Are we to Part like this, Bill.* The choruses are well known to most people, but the descriptive verses are, sadly, seldom heard. Here you will find them telling in eloquent narrative the plaintive or humorous reason for those immediately-recognisable choruses.

The remarkable thing about the songs in this book is that they are still being sung and played after so many years, reminding us of an age when lyrics were poetical and music melodious. How many of today's songs will survive this test of time? In the current climate, dominated by pop music, the publication of this songbook makes a welcome change, and gives a chance for every age group to enjoy 'the songs that father sang and mother listened to'. Here they are, waiting to be played and wanting to be sung.

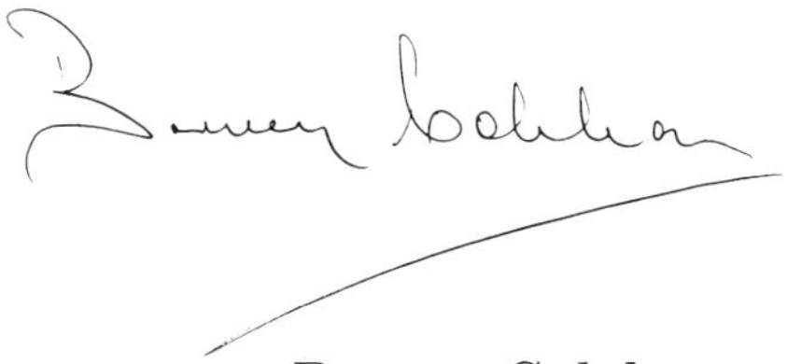

Barney Colehan

Introduction

What were – or are – the 'good old days'? It is not easy to be precise in the matter because good old days tend to merge into one another. Roughly speaking, they start (when we are children) by being the days which our grandparents remembered as they bounced us on their knees. As we get beyond the bouncing age, they become the days that our parents remembered (for by this time they have become grand-parents as well); and, by the time we have become grandparents ourselves, they are the days that were going on when we were aged ten or thereabouts. It should be clear from this that good old days take a long time to mature, that they didn't just happen yesterday, and that they are, in ecclesiastical terms, eminently movable. To the bouncees of the present, inconceivable as it may seem as we survey our morning paper, the days of the soaring-price seventies will some day qualify as good old days.

It's all a bit confusing, particularly when you have to acknowledge that good old days are often, collectively, a part of bad old times. For instance, nobody in his right senses would claim that the years now historically labelled as World Wars I and II were exactly periods of human glory and sanity. Yet many hark back to those days, and the records that remain by way of song and story, and talk of the way people then had a tendency to help their neighbours and generally exhibited a spirit that we find deplorably lacking in these nasty new days. At this very moment somewhere some desperate group of humans is embroiled in some dispute not of its own making and is uniting – and immortalising – its frail spirits in some contemporary equivalent of *Keep the home fires burning* or *Roll out the barrel.*

Now I think we are beginning to put our fingers on to the essence of what made good old days good. They can clearly be divorced from bad old times, when little boys were sent up chimneys and all the monstrous errors of selfishness, greed and fear manifested themselves in poverty and ill-health and all the fearful prejudices of colour, creed and class. They become good old days by virtue of the defiant spirit they created. The evils can never be forgotten because they created the reactionary unpleasantnesses that are with us today. The goodness might also be forgotten if it was not preserved in many forms to satisfy our appetite for nostalgia.

Good old days, embedded in their bad old times, were (at least in distant retrospect) simpler, in that society appeared to accept inequalities: 'The rich man in his castle, / The poor man at his gate: / God made them high or lowly, / And ordered their estate', as Mrs Alexander said in her immortal hymn. And they remained so for so long probably because horizons were so much narrower. There was no way you could switch on the radio or television to see what unpleasant things people were doing at the other end of the earth – or even in the next country. But equally there was no way that such a situation could remain stable, with some having it so good and some having it so bad.

Enough: I intend to let the mud settle and get down to some contemplation of the riches that the good old days have left as their legacy; mainly in the shape of music-hall entertainment and some characters of undiminished glory; running my nostalgic thread of text through the music of sixty songs that stand as undeniable evidence that the good old days were worthy of their name by virtue of the good things they bred.

MR. SLADE MURRAY.

First, let us remind ourselves that 'music hall' as a genre was not confined to a certain golden period which we mentally envisage as happening somewhere between 1860 and 1910. Popular entertainment has a natural habit of adapting itself to whatever means are at its disposal and the current whims of those who happen to be paying for it. It so happened, at some uncertain time long ago, that certain commercially-minded gentlemen who ran popular hostelries saw the need and demand for organised entertainment to which the drinking men of this world could bring their wives. They began to add to their establishments halls, or utilised existing spacious rooms, wherein an entertainment loosely coming under the category of music might be enjoyed – always remembering, of course, that singing tends to make people thirsty. That was the basis of the age of music hall. The type of entertainment heard in those halls was more generally referred to as 'variety' which gives a clear if undefined hint of its intent. The first substantial book to be written on the subject called itself *The Variety Stage*, and saw music hall as simply the collective place where all this happened.

It also so happened that the age that coincided with the growth and spread of music halls (an outward manifestation of working-class spending power) was the age most frequently saddled with the term 'good old days': an age of settled morality, growing affluence and professional wars that didn't bother the general populace too much (they were rather looked upon as test matches, in which it was hoped and expected, then, that England would win). So that the music-hall world of the late nineteenth century has become a symbol of those good old days – like a piece of romantic theatrical scenery which gives no hint of the tawdriness behind it.

That there was always some sort of variety entertainment around is self-evident. Since the beginning of history the wandering minstrels, acrobats, jugglers and lowbrow entertainers had been playing their role in keeping people happy in their leisure hours. They are depicted on Egyptian vases and Chinese toothbrush-holders dating back thousands of years BC. However, nobody pretends that those were good old days, least of all the performers, who were likely to be put in the stocks or even lose portions of their anatomy if their performances were below par. And actors and musicians complain about the modest strictures of today's critics!

In early times the current variety artistes regularly aped the nobility; but this was simply because (as in much opera and operetta) it was only their fairy-tale and well-moneyed world that seemed worth reporting. Shakespeare started a clear trend toward interest in what the inferior classes did and thought, and we gradually become aware that they also liked and needed entertainment—providing it was cheap enough. The first English fairs were the result of worshippers and pilgrims gathering near the abbeys and cathedrals on feast days, and needing something to while away what the package-tour operators would now refer to as their free time. Such was the fair that gradually grew up around the celebrations of the feast of St Bartholomew in the first half of the twelfth century. In the already flourishing Smithfield Market in East London, the Priory of St Bartholomew was founded by a monk named Rayer, formerly a jester in the Court of Henry I, who was given the promotion rights to the fair held on the saint's feast day each autumn. By the early eighteenth century, Bartholomew Fair was well

Bartholomew Fair c. 1799, engraving after a sketch by Thomas Rowlandson; from Henry Morley's Memoirs of Bartholomew Fair *(1899)*

established as an annual riot (in 1719 there were twenty licensed gaming tables allowed); and every kind of entertainer, from ballad singer to freak, abounded and claimed their pitch. The last fair took place in 1855, its death caused by the age-old hazard of inflation. In 1838 rents had been doubled, until finally only a few well-to-do suppliers of gingerbreads could afford the fee; and seven centuries of riotous tradition came to an end.

Bartholomew Fair had some hand in formulating the type of entertainment that was to become the staple diet of the music hall. So did the innumerable penny gaffs of the nineteenth century: makeshift theatres where the patrons sat on wooden benches, paying a penny to see what could mainly be described (to be generous) as 'legitimate' theatre entertainment, of the lowest standard. The same was true of the various pleasure gardens, spas and coffee-houses that flourished in and around London. The better-class gardens (which were nevertheless the venue for many unseemly frolics in their ornamental acres) tended to present fairly highbrow entertainment. Vauxhall Gardens, which opened in 1728, started out in ambitious style as a place of beauty and culture. It was decorated by Hogarth's paintings and the music was supplied by a regular orchestra and an organ (played on by Handel) and by the services of all the leading musicians of the day. Gradually

The Penny Gaff. Engraving by Phiz from James Grant's Sketches in London *(1838)*

VAUXHALL—WHERE SLOMAN SANG.

Vauxhall succumbed to the general tendency toward brow-lowering, as its custom presumably became more middle, and eventually lower, class, and it began to mix firework displays and balloon ascents with popular musical programmes and gala performances. Eventually it lost its identity and closed in 1859.

Various theatres after 1800, mainly in the East End of London or some south-of-the-river haunt, began to put on shows which were a rudimentary mixture of music-hall and penny-gaff entertainment. They offered enormous, spectacular programmes which give an impression of aimlessness: performing dogs, followed by operatic prima donnas, intermingled with scenic tableaux. The quandary of the popular theatre was the identity of its customers. This is reflected in the extraordinary programmes devised, so it seems, to please both the earls on the rampage and the poor who had come in out of the cold.

One of the strong rivals to Vauxhall was Cremorne in Chelsea, which finally gave in to the urban developer in 1877. On a smaller scale there were innumerable 'tea gardens', providing open-air drinking in the summer months and indoor dancing-saloons and concert rooms in the winter; places with picturesque names and low reputations like Jenny's Whim near Ebury Bridge, which started as a sort of miniature Vauxhall but had become an ordinary tavern by 1804 and was pulled down in 1865. There was the Old Milestone, situated where Goswell Street now runs, the White Conduit House in Clerkenwell where the famous Charles Sloman, 'improvisatore', first made his reputation; and where John Dunn, 'the English Jim Crow', who based his art on that of the celebrated T. D. Rice, acted as chairman around 1840. Bagnigge Wells in the Pentonville Road area disappeared in 1841, and Highbury Barn in 1861.

In the bad old days, entertainment was very much an *ad hoc* affair; the entertainers got what tips they could, depending on their own efforts and the consequent generosity of the patrons, with perhaps a few free drinks from the proprietors of the establishments they performed in. Of the popular writers and composers of the period we know next to nothing.

The beginnings of the good old days of variety entertainment, as it welded itself into the collective phenomenon of 'music hall', were manifested in a new commercial organisation. It became a proper business with recognised outlets. The discovery of cheap ways of printing music led to the founding of music-publishing businesses, which would now print the popular ditties that had before been passed on in performance, with no possible profit to their anonymous creators. But it was no good printing music until people could cheaply possess the means to play it, so a parallel industry in musical instruments grew up. In the 1830s you could buy a good parlour piano for around twelve guineas. It was the growing affluence (if you could fairly call it that) of working and lower-middle-class people that created not only a good Saturday-night clientèle, but one which increasingly wanted organised entertainment every night of the week. As the premises to provide this became established and profitable, the management had to pay more to get the best entertainers, and the entertainers had to pay more to get the best songwriters to provide material for them – and all of them found that they needed agents to look after their affairs, and eventually associations to protect their interests. And so entertainment became a business – but that is the unmentionably sordid side of the whole thing.

The organisation that grew into the world of music hall began in the early 1800s as a logical step from the scattered entertainments that we have already briefly mentioned. The proprietors of the larger inns, taverns and other forerunners of the good old British 'public house', acting in concerted rivalry, saw that they had to have a sizeable music-room attached to their premises where some sort of organised entertainment could be presented. This attracted drinking customers and their families. Some of the halls became more important than the pubs to which they were attached and it was but a step to start building special halls and eventually theatres where you could have a drink with your entertainment, rather than rooms where you could have some entertainment with your drink.

The process was hastened and formalised by the parallel development of premises which were not exactly pubs and not exactly theatres. Known as song-and-supper rooms, they began to flourish around the 1830s. They grew up all over London but the best-known ones flourished in an area of the West End in and around the Strand. In all but name they were variety theatres with a small stage on which an assortment of vocal and comic entertainment went on under the chairmanship of a popular host who would probably provide some of the entertainment himself, and ribald remarks in the meantime. In the early days it was on an amateur basis, with regulars of talent called from the hall to entertain. Gradually the better performers with pleasing talents were offered a retaining fee and quite quickly the whole enterprise had established a professional basis. The big

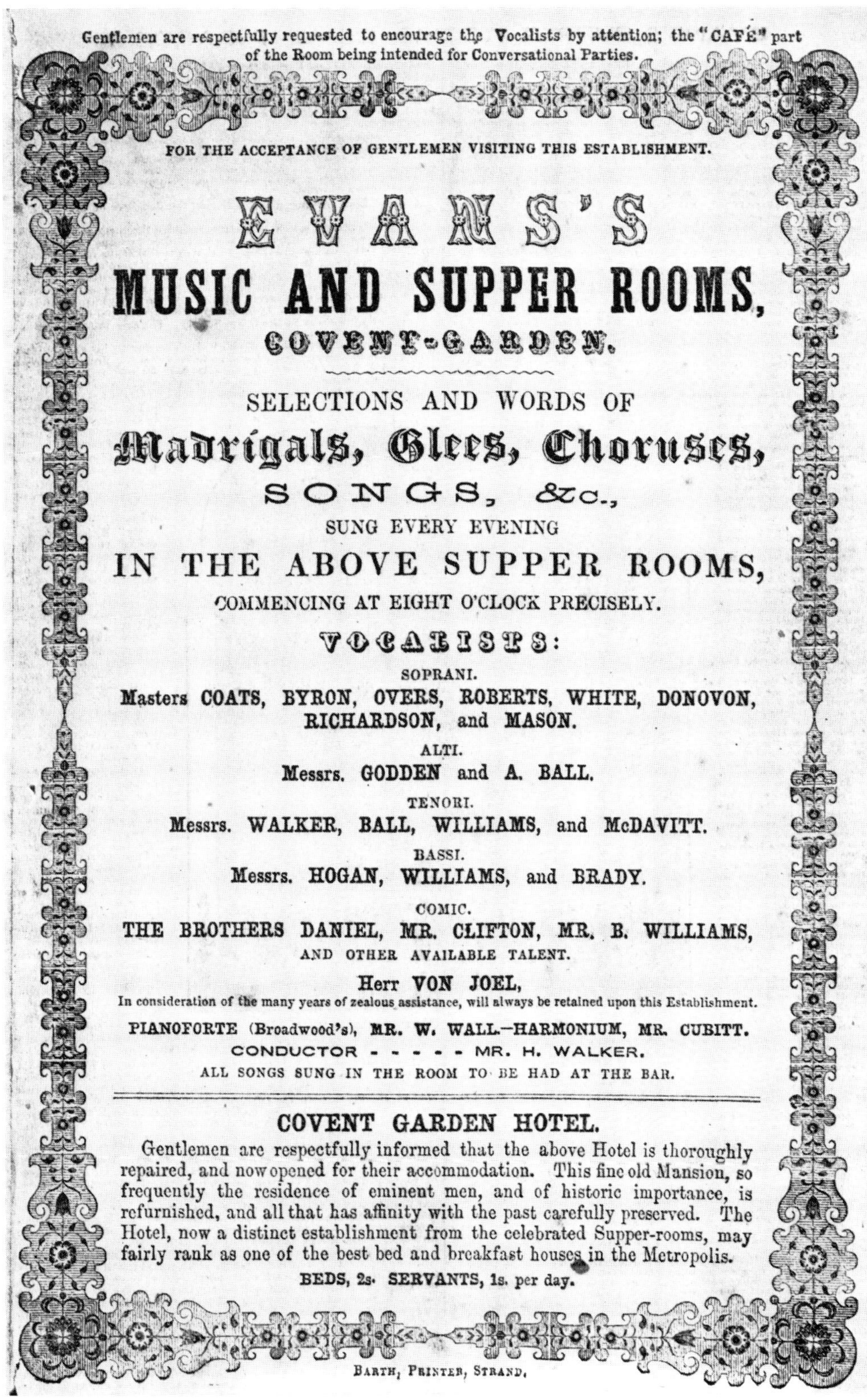

difference between song-and-supper rooms and theatres was that the patrons went there to seat themselves at tables and enjoy a first-rate hot supper accompanied by a tankard of ale or a glass of grog amid a convivial atmosphere of rowdy good nature and cigar smoke. On the whole, the song-and-supper rooms catered for the better-off who could afford to spend lavishly: professional gentlemen, literary men like Mr Thackeray who was a well-known frequenter, and those of private means. It was essentially a male world, though ladies were gradually allowed provided they could offer a good address or some evidence of male attachment; but even then they were kept behind rails on a balcony or in some separate part of the establishment. To begin with the entertainment had quite an elevated character about it. Glees and madrigals were performed from the floor with elaborate books of words on sale, which also offered a remarkable range of potted culture in their numerous pages. The entertainment gradually descended toward music-hall level as the professional entertainers took over with their wider abilities in perpetrating the difficult art of comedy.

MR. G. W. HUNTER.

The leading establishment was the one that had its most flourishing period as Evans's, situated in a fine old house at 43 King Street in Covent Garden. The house had originally been built in elaborate style during the reign of Charles II, and had been inhabited by successive members of the peerage. It began its social downfall in 1773 when it was turned into a family hotel, one of the first of its kind in London. As such it passed through the hands of various proprietors until it was taken over by a Mr Joy and, as Joy's Hotel, took on more of the nature of an aristocratic West End Club, much patronised by the aristocracy and with an impressive dining-room where the Establishment frequently gathered. So elevated was the company that the room became known as The Star: 'It was no uncommon thing for nine dukes to be dining there on one day'. It was also the meeting place of the Institute of British Architects. The next proprietor was Mr W. C. Evans who traded under the name of 'Evans's (late Joys)' – the last part of the title, 'Late Joys', being neatly adapted in later years for a popular revival of the song-and-supper tradition under the arches at Charing Cross, now known as the Players Theatre. Evans turned the famous dining-room into a music-and-supper room and let out the upper rooms as flats. Opening at midnight it became a well-to-do establishment for dining and singing bawdy songs (some of which were very bawdy indeed).

In 1844 Mr Evans retired and the management was taken over by the popular chairman and entertainer – who also had connections with the Adelphi Theatre and Covent Garden Opera – Paddy Green. Under his guidance the premises were entirely rebuilt with a new hall some seventy-two feet long and complete with stage and separate accommodation for ladies; the old dining-room, still used as a restaurant, now formed a vestibule to the main room. It was splendidly appointed with a carved and painted ceiling and ornamented pillars along its sides behind which was a screened gallery for the fair sex. It cost some £20,000 to carry out the alterations, and there was now seating

MR. HARRY RANDALL.

capacity for 1000. The rest of the premises operated as the Covent Garden Hotel.

Performances now began at eight and went on till around two in the morning, always presided over with dictatorial benevolence by Mr Paddy Green. The accounts were settled at the door where a well-known character called Skinner did some quick mental arithmetic and, in the general confusion, achieved totals that were grossly in favour of himself and the management. The first 'pros' to entertain there were attracted from the pleasure gardens and public saloons. There was Jones the bass from Drury Lane and Binge the tenor from Vauxhall. The first well-known comic to make a name at Evans's was Jack Sharp, previously known at such establishments as the Old Mogul and The Grapes in Compton Street. He was paid £1 a week, an average fee, plus free supper and drinks, and as much as he could make on the side from the sale of song-sheets and tips. Many of the songs were written by a John Labern, whose history is otherwise undocumented. Sharp achieved a terrific reputation and appeared at all the main pleasure gardens but, like many artistes in those days, the hard toil and the drink had their effect and he died in 1856, only thirty-eight, in the Dover Workhouse. Charles Sloman was another great favourite for his ability to improvise lines of doggerel on any suggested name or subject. Sam Cowell, the singer of *The Rat-Catcher's Daughter* and other ditties which achieved phenomenal sales, and who later toured the early halls with his own company, was a regular at Evans's for a time. There was a yodelling German called Herr von Joel who supplemented his income by selling cigars; Tom 'One-Eyed' Martin and many other colourful characters. After Paddy Green's days the place survived under other managers and became respectable enough to admit ladies on an equal footing. After its song-and-supper days were over it became the Grand Hotel in 1854, the Falstaff Club in 1880 and eventually the National Sporting Club.

Another favourite room from the 1820s was the Coal Hole in Fountain Court off the Strand. There is still a tavern of the same name nearby although the original premises gave way to Terry's Theatre. There a Mr John Rhodes provided food in grand style and introduced such entertainers as Charles Sloman, Joe Wells – a singer of bawdy songs, and Ben Mills, all of whom drifted from establishment to establishment. Immortalised as the 'Cave of Harmony' by Thackeray, it was run by Rhodes until he died in 1850 and, at the end of its brief career, by John Bruton from Vauxhall Gardens. It was closed and demolished when the Strand was widened.

At No 20 Maiden Lane there was a place known as the Cyder Cellars, with a long history behind it of low-class entertainment, excellent food, good brandy and stout, and the cider which gave it the name. It was here that the celebrated W. G. Ross sang his crudely dramatic songs, including the notorious *Sam Hall*, a brutal and blasphemous ditty which made a great impression on all who heard it. On the strength of it Mr Ross made quite a bit on the side by selling unedifying portraits of himself. Sloman appeared here as well as a very well-known vocalist called Tom Hudson who wrote and sang his own songs. These, in their way, were literary masterpieces that added such catchwords as *Jack Robinson* (of 'before you could say' . . . fame) to the English language. He also wrote the original *The Spider and the Fly* but he died in poverty in 1844. The Cyder Cellars closed in 1862 when a licence was finally refused.

Another thriving establishment was the Dr Johnson Hotel Supper and City Concert Rooms in Bolt Court off Fleet Street, which attracted all the previously mentioned artistes and many more beside. One of the music-hall artistes of later repute who made her professional début there was Jenny Hill, who became known as 'The Vital Spark'. A famous chairman was actor and songwriter John Caulfield, who later worked for Charles Morton at the Canterbury and Oxford Music Halls. The Dr Johnson eventually became the City Music Hall which survived until 1863, and in 1895 it became a sporting establishment known as the Albert Club.

The song-and-supper rooms helped to create the fraternity of entertainers who found further outlet and increased reward in the variety saloons and concert rooms attached to the well-known taverns which began to flourish in mid-century. These saloons were licensed by the authorities to produce almost anything except, for some odd reason, Shakespeare – presumably to keep the pride of English literature in an unblemished state. A mixture of melodrama, opera and miscellaneous turns gradually evolved into something like the typical music-hall bill of later days. The big difference between these places and the song-and-supper rooms was that they tended to cater for a lower-class and lower-paid clientele. The fare consisted of drinks and light snacks rather than elaborate hot meals.

One of the grandest and best-known of these music-rooms was the one attached to the Eagle Tavern in Shepherdess Walk off the City Road—immortalised in the popular song *Pop goes the Weasel.* The room of entertainment had been built separately in the gardens of the Eagle in 1825, and was known from 1832–46 as the Grecian Saloon. It was rebuilt as the Grecian Theatre in 1858, with a sizeable stage, boxes for the more affluent customers and a permanent organ, with an orchestra pit added in 1876. Its entertainments were originally ambitious enough to include full-length ballets and productions of operas including *La Sonnambula*, and it was here that the great tenor Sims Reeves made his early reputation. The entertainment gradually inclined toward variety. The theatre closed in 1882 but music-hall entertainment continued at the Eagle Tavern Music Hall (sometime known as the Royal Eagle) in a large room holding 300 on the first floor of the tavern, until 1887. On similar lines was the Union Saloon in Shoreditch and the Britannia Saloon in Hoxton, which had a spacious hall at the rear of its main building where many later celebrated artists made their early appearances. Such places now sprang up like mushrooms. There was the Albion Saloon at the rear of the Yorkshire Stingo in Marylebone; the Bower in Stangate Street; the Albert Saloon in Shepherdess Walk, Hoxton; the Effingham Saloon in the Whitechapel Road.

The move toward legitimate music hall was hastened by the authorities when they tried to regularise the entertainment world by passing the Theatres Registry Act in 1843. In order to leave no loopholes they included all saloons and music halls in the rulings and decreed that these should be run as and described as theatres within the letter of the law. They were left to decide whether to turn themselves into legitimate theatres licensed to produce plays (including Shakespare) but with no drinking allowed in the auditorium; to become music halls which were licensed to sell drinks to the audience but were not allowed to produce straight plays; or to revert to their old role as plain taverns. The Grecian and the Britannia in 1858 both became legitimate theatres. Most of the others opted for the choice that put them on the way to being proper music halls. These included The Grapes in Southwark, the King's Head in Knightsbridge, the Rose of Normandy in Marylebone, the New Inn in Westminster Road, the Raglan in Theobald's Road, the Royal Standard in Vauxhall Bridge Road and the Swan Tavern which was somewhere where Charing Cross station now stands. Some of these now produced permanent weekly bills of fare, with bookable tickets and reasonably well-paid entertainers. The variety stage was now established.

It is difficult to decide which establishment deserves the title of the first music hall. One of the earliest places to provide variety entertainment in a theatrical manner (with food and drink not a first consideration) was the Old Rotunda Assembly Rooms in Blackfriars Road. In 1829, fifteen or so years before anywhere else was doing it, the Old Rotunda presented variety bills with stars such as Charles Sloman and Mr and Mrs Johnny Wilde (parents of Dan Leno). The first of the public-house rooms to call itself a music hall and behave like one was The Grapes in the Southwark Bridge Road. After styling itself the British Saloon and the Grand Harmonic Hall, it took on the title of the Surrey Music Hall in the early 1840s and boasted a 'theatre' capable of seating 2000 and a regular orchestra and musical director. Louie Sherrington and Willie and Emma Ward, were among its favourite entertainers. It later became known as the Winchester Music Hall, under which title it was demolished in 1878. By then a new Surrey Music Hall, built in the Surrey Zoological Gardens near Kennington Park in 1856, was flourishing (seating capacity almost 10,000). It was destroyed by fire in 1861 and was remodelled as the Surrey Gardens Theatre in 1872.

The Great Mogul had its saloon altered and enlarged in 1847 and became known as the Middlesex Music Hall from 1851 to 1911 under the original management of Edwin Winder (who later also converted the White Lion in the Edgware Road into the Metropolitan Music Hall). The Middlesex became a true music hall, and was rebuilt in 1872 and enlarged several times after that in response to the rising popularity of music hall as an entertainment. From 1911 to 1919 it was known as the New Middlesex Theatre of Varieties and from 1919 to 1960 as the Winter Garden Theatre. In 1965 it was demolished. With the Middlesex we move into the mainstream of music-hall history. Harry Fox was one of its early stars and it was here that Dan Leno first made his reputation as a comedian. A famous chairman was Gus Leach.

The halls went through their own period of becoming respectable. Gradually they became family fare, as the new halls were built on elegant and comfortable lines and the law took a hand in inducing respectability. One of the first to establish the music hall as a place of family entertainment, indeed to make a point of it, was the Canterbury

Hall in the Westminster Bridge Road, opened in 1851 by Charles Morton, who was later to rejoice in the title of 'Father of the Halls'. It was built on ground at the back of the Canterbury Tavern (an ancient inn site) which Morton acquired in 1848. It accommodated 700, admission was charged, and a general variety bill was given on a large platform under the chairmanship of John Caulfield and the musical direction of Mr Jonghmann. At this stage of music-hall history

Morton was paying his top artistes as much as £30 a week, and was thus able to command the services of such popular men as Sam Cowell and E. W. Mackney. The variety bill was interspersed with concerts of classical music and operatic excerpts by leading 'serious' singers and the Canterbury did capacity business. Such was the success and the demand that a new hall was built in 1854 (being ingeniously erected over the old one so that the performances could continue) and there was now accommodation for 1500, well lighted and surrounded by a balcony. The entrance fee shot up to ninepence in the gallery and sixpence in the stalls. A constant flow of music was provided between acts on piano and harmonium and a chairman still presided. As described in Ritchie's *The Night Side of London*:

> The room is crowded and almost every gentleman has a pipe or a cigar in his mouth. Evidently the majority present are respectable mechanics or small tradesmen with their wives and daughters and sweethearts. Now and then you see a midshipman, or a few fast clerks and warehousemen. Everyone is smoking, and everyone has a glass before him; but the class that come here are economical, and chiefly confine themselves to pipes and porter.

A far cry from the lavish spending in the song-and-supper rooms.

In 1876 yet another bigger and better Canterbury was built, taking in the sites of several adjoining houses, 100 by 70 ft in size and costing over £40,000 to build. It had a sliding roof that could be opened in hot weather. By this time the Canterbury's stars included such immortal names as George Leybourne (who arrived, by way of advertisement, in a carriage and pair provided by the management, and seriously promoted champagne – with *Champagne Charlie* – and other drinks in modern style), the Great Vance, Fred Coyne, Arthur Roberts, James Fawn and Nelly Power. In between the variety shows it still provided serious entertainment and was known for the best ballet in London. Royalty were frequent visitors. It was destroyed in 1942.

The success of the Canterbury naturally influenced the opening of other specialised halls and the great music-hall boom was on. The Euston (later Frampton's) was another place of high repute which seated 1000 and opened in Duke's Row, St Pancras, in 1852, but it only survived until 1862, by which time it was known as the Lord Nelson. Wilton's in Stepney was opened in 1858. A fire halted activities in 1877 and it ceased to be a music hall in 1879, when it failed to comply with the 1878 regulations of the Metropolitan Board of Works. The building still stands, and various attempts have been made in recent years to turn it into a revival music hall. The Rose of Normandy became a legitimate music hall in 1858 under the name of the Marylebone and the management of the Irish comedian Sam Collins. The Philharmonic in Islington was founded in 1860 and gave its last variety shown in 1932 as the Islington Empire. The Lord Raglan, in Theobalds Road, flourished from 1855 to 1878, being closed, like its namesake in Plumstead, by the

1878 act. The Trevor (1854–89) and the Sun (1851–91) were both in Knightsbridge. The East End was full of short-lived halls. The only one to challenge the overall popularity of the Canterbury was Weston's in Holborn, opened in 1857, which had a long and successful history, ending up as the Holborn Empire, before being closed by bombs in 1941.

The second generation of halls starts with the new decade and the South London Music Hall, which opened in December 1860 and was more like a modern theatre. In 1861 this architectural trend towards music halls built like legitimate theatres was again followed in the first Oxford Music Hall on the site of the Boar and Castle in Oxford Street. It had a sad history of being burnt down, destroyed by fire in 1868, rising from the ashes again in 1869. It was burned down again in 1872 and was rebuilt yet again in 1873. Its final rebuilding in 1893 turned it into a modern variety theatre. Also in 1861 the Bedford Theatre, another little gem in traditional style, red plush and gilt, proper proscenium and pit, was built in Camden Town High Street. It was used as a music hall until 1950 and was demolished in 1963. And the same year of 1861 saw the opening of Deacon's Music Hall, which was demolished in 1891 for the construction of Rosebery Avenue. Collins' opened in Islington in 1862 behind the Lansdowne Arms, and closed as the result of a fire in 1958. There were the great palaces of variety like the Alhambra and the Trocadero, and a flood of building and rebuilding that saw some 100 halls open in London, and almost as many in other parts of the country. The last genuine surviving music hall in London was probably the Metropolitan in the Edgware Road, opened as a concert room in 1836, rebuilt as a theatre in 1864 and finally closing its doors in 1962.

Let us now turn the clock back 100 years and more, landing ourselves comfortably in the 'good old days' of 1860 or thereabouts, and go on a 'bachelor' jaunt to London:

Intending to make a night of it on the Saturday and to visit some of the Pleasure Gardens on the Sunday, we have booked a hotel for the night by letter. An uncle, who makes frequent jaunts of this nature, has recommended Edwards's Private Hotel at 23 Norfolk Street. We arrive at Charing Cross soon after nine and, having a few items of luggage with us, take a cab to our hotel which lies beyond Somerset House and the Waterloo Bridge. On mentioning Uncle Albert's recommendation we are warmly greeted by Mr Edwards himself and shown comfortable rooms overlooking the river, already a busy and exciting scene on that sunny morning with a constant succession of steamers and other craft passing up and down, an entertainment in itself. Well worth the three shillings per person that we are paying for bed and breakfast. We deposit our bags, wash, and set out to shop and explore, having been warned by our host to keep to the main thoroughfares and not to wander down any narrow alleys, especially after dark when they bristle with footpads and all kinds of rogues ready to waylay respectable citizens.

We decide to do our shopping in the morning. Both of us require

some shirts. I buy half a dozen ready made, being of accommodating size, at the establishment of a Mr Lewis Jacobs (late Fuggle) at a shop a few doors West of Somerset House, at a cost of thirty-seven shillings and sixpence. My friend, being of less average build, finds nothing there to fit him and visits Laurence's in Southampton Street where his requirements are suited. We visit a newsagent in the Strand where James purchases his copy of *The Eclipse and Sporting Calendar* and I sample a copy of the new penny weekly periodical *Town Talk* – a well-filled and diverting journal of social, literary, theatrical and political gossip. We spend some time at Ponders' Cigar shop, almost opposite the Lowther Arcade, and buy a pound of good foreign Havanas for twenty-five shillings and two-hundred-and-fifty No 2 Government Manilla Cheroots for two-guineas. I also decide to stock up with a half-pound of Ponders' Havana Birds Eye Tobacco (two shillings and eightpence) and am persuaded to try one of Pilliner's new Cabalistic Colouring Pipes (one shilling in a case) which I am assured give an enchanting flavour to all tobaccos. We call at Holloway's the chemist to take back for the family medical cupboard a jar of Holloway's Ointment and some Keating's Cough Lozenges. Finding time running out we hasten to Leicester Square where I know I can get some song books that I want. Tempted by an array of delights at Dyer's in Princes Street, we purchase *Labern's Comic Songster* and *Sharp's New Comic Songster* at 2/6 each (knowing they will cost more if we get them at Evans's later) and the *Cremorne Song Book* at the same price. Also a copy of *The Lady of the Camellias* which costs one shilling and twopence, handsomely bound. We take a cab to Simpson's where we enjoy an excellent repast of roast beef washed down with some of their best ale.

Comfortably put into a cultural frame of mind we have ourselves taken to Dr Kahn's Museum & Gallery of Science in Tichbourne Street near the Haymarket where it is fascinating to peruse the newest discoveries in Natural Philosophy, the startling results of Electricity, the mighty wonders of Magnetism (all illustrated by brilliant and imposing experiments), the pre-Adamite marvels of Geology, the Solar System perfectly illustrated by Guenal's new Orrery, the Oxy-Hydrogen Microscope – not to forget Dr Kahn's special display of Anatomical and Pathological Preparations. I must say that the whole display is most fascinating to any studious and reflecting person in conveying to the mind an exact idea of the human frame and the principles of vitality. It is all done in a way calculated not to offer the slightest shock to the most modest temperament. At six we attend a lecture by Dr Kahn himself on the Human Frame, the Laws of Life and the Preservation of Health which is most educative. As it is growing dark by the time we leave we are able to appreciate the effectiveness of Du Bosque's magnificent electric light which illuminates the outside of the building.

We are tempted to visit the Royal Colosseum to hear Dr Bachhoffner's celebrated illustrative lecture on Donati's Comet but decide to forgo that pleasure until the morrow. So we return to our hotel for a wash and other requirements and, after some light refreshment in the lounge, send a boy out to get us a cab for our much-looked-forward-to visit to Evans's. We are glad to arrive at the door by transport it is well known that the market porters, a gang of cutpurses and pugilists for the most part, are inclined to waylay solitary foot passengers. We are welcomed at the door by the genial proprietor Paddy Green, with his distinguished white hair and rubicund countenance, as if we were his greatest friends. At the same time one senses that he has taken a quick estimate of our financial soundness. Seated at our tables we feel comfortably at ease in what one can only describe as gentlemanly surroundings of real comfort and high quality. Around the walls are the priceless oil paintings belonging to the Garrick, situated here since that historical building suffered damage by fire. The gas lights flicker on a rich scene, already mellowed by cigar smoke. The crystal chandeliers, though no longer bearing their candles, glitter; a veritable army-corps of waiters, including a battalion of boys in buttons, hover ready to give us every immediate attention. Where could one be better placed than in this fine house of entertainment, well built, well conducted and well ventilated? We allow ourselves to be introduced to traditional Evans's fare; a finely done steak, the obligatory potato brought in its skin in a clean white napkin, gently kneaded by the venerable waiter till all its particles are loosened, broken and the hemispheres rubbed together till the smoking, floury delight is on the plate. A dusty bottle of the finest wine from ancient cellars. Followed by the best welsh rabbit in the country and a tankard of porter, with a flask of brandy twinkling on the table awaiting the courtesy of accompanying good cigars sold to us by the aged Von Joel who, as the programme mentioned, 'in consideration of many years of zealous assistance, will always be retained upon this Establishment'; the doddery old singer and siffleur uses his aged charms to sell us the very same *Comic Songsters* we had bought in the morning and left at the hotel – at a considerably inflated price.

By now Mr Green has the entertainment in process starting with a selection of madrigals, glees and choruses sung by a mixed male group of men and boys, about twenty in number, with a Mr Wall at the Broadwood's Pianoforte, a Mr Cubitt at the Harmonium and a Mr H. Walker conducting. The audience join in and we could move nearer to the main hall, where 'total attention' is requested, but we prefer to stay at the comfort of our table where 'conversational parties' are permissible. Among the entertainers we enjoy some very amusing musical antics by the Brothers Daniel, some songs of mingled uplift and humour by the handsome Mr Clifton and some broader humour from a certain Mr B. Williams. Even Herr Joel is prevailed upon to perform. We retain only the haziest recollections of the conclusion of our visit at around half-past one and of being relieved of what seems a rather exorbitant amount of money by an ineffable character at the door, of being poured in and out of a cab, and resuming some sort of consciousness, thankfully, in our Norfolk Street hotel. The next day is overcast and very wet, so we cut short our visit and return to the calm of the country . . . .

Next we might visit the Canterbury Music Hall around 1870; less of a social occasion and more of a well-meaning attempt to mingle with the lower classes. Elegant and well-apportioned the Canterbury certainly is, and we sit in comfort in a Private Box at two guineas, which gives us entrée to the Grand Lounge; but there is not the same emphasis on good living. Drinks and cold victuals are available, but they have none of the mellowed charm of those to be had at Evans's. Even the waiters have more of a hired-for-the-evening look about them. Still, this is no longer the age of affluent gentlemen paying scant attention to underpaid singers. We are about to be allowed into the presence of elegant entertainers earning princely amounts of over £20 a week, and frequently given priority by the cabbies. (Actually, we came here in a horse-drawn bus as cabs are beginning to get a bit expensive.)

We sit and address ourselves to our drinks and anonymous pie as the orchestra under the dignified direction of M. Edouard Frewin plays us the Overture from Monsieur Auber's splendid opera *Masaniello*. It wears its fifty years well, but barely subdues our chatter. The variety bill opens with Musical Character Sketches by Miss Essel May and Mr Henry Verrall, which are only lightly amusing and promote a few ribald remarks from the Hall and Promenade clientèle. We find that one of the stars of the evening is next to appear, but we understand that having numerous other engagements to fill around the town he has made this his early night at the Canterbury. Mr George Leybourne is a man of dignified presence. Although he started out as a mechanic named Joe Saunders, he now looks at least a member of the House of Lords. Extremely handsome and blessed with a rich voice, he is only in his late twenties; though experience and good living has given him the appearance of twice that age. Indeed you might say that he looks a bit tired, if his zest and confidence were not amply able to overcome such suggestion. We are in the presence of a household name who even has his own private song to introduce him; a growing fashion in the halls we believe. He sings of the glories and rewards of drinking champagne in an already well-known piece called *Champagne Charlie*, which he wrote in 1866 and for which (so it is said) Moët's, the champagne manufacturers, reward him with a handsome supply of free magnums. He then charms us with an amusing ditty, *The daring young man on the flying trapeze*, which is inspired by that intrepid acrobat Monsieur Léotard, recently seen at the Alhambra. Mr Leybourne mashes us with a saucy joke or two in a well-feigned upper-class drawl, and then takes us by surprise by launching into a popular sentimental ballad which he sings in remarkably good style. After which he assumes a slightly tipsy stance and launches into a song in praise of wine – for which we assume some grateful wine company is handing out crates. Mr Leybourne could well leave it at that and hurry off to his next appointment, but he is well loved by the balcony and promenade clientèle, who like to get their full sixpennyworth or shillingsworth (according to proximity). They persuade him, with not too much effort, to sing his latest hit, inspired by the siege of Paris, which tells of the thrills of going 'up in a

Programme

For week ending AUG. 10th.

THE CANTERBURY

LICENSED UNDER THE 25TH OF GEO II. TO F. VILLIERS.

THE SLIDING ROOF

Designed and Patented by Mr. E. VILLIERS, is opened every evening, weather permitting, thus securing complete ventilation to the auditorium.

PRICES OF ADMISSION.

Private Boxes ...	...£1 1s. and £2 2s.
Numbered Fauteuils (Reserved) ...	... 5s.
Orchestra Stalls	... 3s.
The Patrons of the above have Entrée to the Grand Lounge.	
Balcony and Promenade	... 2s.
Hall and Promenade	... 1s.
Upper Balcony	... 6d.

The Box Office at the Canterbury is open daily from 10 to 4 o'clock, where Seats, with no Fees for Booking, may be secured by letter, telegram, or personal application.

THIS PROGRAMME IS SUBJECT TO ALTERATION.

Stage Manager:

MR. J. TRESSIDDER.

Maitre de Ballet:

M. DEWINNE.

Musical Director:

M. EDOUARD FREWIN.

The Charge for this Programme is TWOPENCE, *and any extra demand made or accepted is requested to be reported to the Management.*

Printed by Letts Son and Co. Limited, 33, King William Street, E.C.

balloon'. Mr Leybourne gracefully departs and one hears his coach and pair clip-clopping away into the night. It is difficult for Miss Rose Lesseur who follows, billed as a 'serio-comic', to make much of an impression after Mr Leybourne, but presumably she is modestly paid to fill this arduous space – and not to be too funny anyway, because she soon gives way to yet another comedian, a Mr Fred Coyne. He works on a lower social stratum than Mr Leybourne but portrays a comic character that has brought him almost equal renown in the various halls of the metropolis.

This initial burst of comedy is obviously intended to put the audience in a good humour for the more serious part of the evening. For the Canterbury is very concerned about its high tone and, believing that its elaborate and high-flown entertainments are what draw the public, it retains them for the climax. After Miss Hilton has sung a song about her love life, a Signor Carlo Benedetti enthralls us all, and whets our appetite, by swallowing a sword no less than thirty inches long. Hailed as 'the wonder of the world for the last five years' and 'the greatest natural phenomenon of the age' he is no doubt what some of the audience were waiting for. After that we are allowed a short interval to refill our glasses.

During our break the stage has taken on the fanciful appearance of a fairy dell dramatically enhanced by amazing electrical effects achieved by the Phospho-Electric Company (patented), under the personal direction of their General Manager, Redmund Barrett. It says so in the programme. We are charmed and diverted by a Fairy Sketch, written by Frank W. Green, called 'The Night Dancers *or* The Little Prince Who Couldn't Keep his Head above Water'. The lead is Prince Rupert of Rheinstein – a Prince who seeks the Rhine for its Rhino. He is the Pet of the Fairies, and (we trust also) the Public, and is played by a charming and curvaceous lady in scanty male disguise, who has a popular following among the audience: Miss Nelly Power. She is delightful, and delivers some unfunny lines with gentle wit. The other main characters in the 'play' are Peppitypop (his servant, a dumb waiter) played without much difficulty, or much effect, by Mr Bertram; and Coraline (Queen of the Night Dancers, of Rupert's Heart, and everybody else's), prettily if not dramatically played by Mlle Bartoletti. The slight plot is nicely padded out by hordes of Water Nymphs and Dolphins with some adorable danseurs, Mlles Phillis Broughton, Florence Powell, M. Carlos and M. Adolphe, under the direction of Maître de Ballet M. H. Dewinne. It must be added that the whole of the music was composed and arranged by M. Edouard Frewin.

You might well think we have had our money's worth after all that, but after a further ten minutes' interval (during which harp solos are played in the Grottoes by Mr Stirling Jones) we still have Mr Fred Wilson doing his Classic Pictures and Characters of Nations; vocal duets by Mlle Katrini and M. Frank Angell, and a final ballet sketch entitled 'Northern Stars' (arranged Dewinne, composed Frewin, in mellifluous harness) with Mlles Broughton, Powell, Carlos, Bertram and Ada and other Ladies of the Corps de Ballet giving a thoroughly cultural finale to our evening. We tiptoe out during the 'pas de quatre' to make sure we don't miss the last omnibus to Clapham Junction. . . .

Let another decade pass, and now we might visit the fine new Variety Theatre known as the Oxford, to find that the whole aspect of music-hall entertainment has taken yet another step into professionalism. We are now in a well-appointed theatre with impressive auditorium and stage with a sizeable orchestra under the direction of the Manager, Mr J. H. Jennings. We are expected to pay strict attention to the artistes, whose names are lavishly billed outside, and our drinking is expected to be fairly silent. Incidentally, the Oxford Wine Carte is excellent, with a range of five clarets from 2/– to 6/– a bottle, old crusted port 6/– a bottle, champagnes 6/– to 10/– a bottle, Chablis at 4/–, Sherries, Burgundy, Moselles, Hocks and Sauternes. And the Public are respectfully invited to call the attention of the Manager, Mr J. H. Jennings (presumably when he is not conducting), to any irregularity on the part of the waiters, who flit quietly to and fro among the little tables, serving refreshments. We smoke our cigarettes – Richmond Gems, Player's Navy Cut or Morris's Compressed, and peruse the advertisements in the programme: Hennig the Billiard people – ('old balls adjusted or exchanged'). Aha! – morning coats at Baker's 29/6; trousers 10/–. Oldridge's Balm of Columbia – 'the best and only certain remedy ever discovered for Preserving, Strengthening, Beautifying or Restoring the HAIR, WHISKERS or MOUSTACHES, and preventing them turning grey – for Children it is invaluable, as it forms the basis of a magnificent head of hair, and prevents baldness in mature age' – yes indeed!

We note that the auditorium has been redecorated at enormous expense by Messrs Worrall & Co., that the new scenery and Act Drop have been painted by E. G. Banks of the Gaiety Theatre. Figures are by G. H. Banks and upholstery by Messrs Shoolbred & Co. We fold up our *Bell's Life in London* – 'the Oldest and the Leading Sporting Paper in the World' – savour our Moselle, and sit back as the Orchestra (under the harassed Mr Jennings, who has probably had to deal with some irregular waiters) launch into the Overture to 'Martha' by Flotow. There is a noisy gallery tonight, as you would expect on a Saturday, and the first act ('a re-engagement of Mr George Sanford, basso-profundo, with fresh songs') is punctuated with jocular remarks about 'singing in his boots' and 'busting his braces'. However, he performs his opening task nobly; and the next act so fills the stage with noise and action that the audience are overwhelmed: Bryant's Minstrels – Marionettes (*par excellence*), Lilliputian Actors, Comedians and Singers – a show in itself, which takes off the popular minstrel shows of Islington and elsewhere and leaves everyone in good and timely humour for the next act. Chirgwin the White-Eyed Musical Kaffir is nothing of the sort, really. George Chirgwin is one of six perfectly white brothers. For many years he appeared as a double act with his brother Jack, but first had a solo success at this very hall, the Oxford, in 1878. His white eyepatch, grotesque in his black make-up, happened by

MORTON'S FIRST OXFORD MUSIC HALL, 1861.

accident one night when he was wiping a fly out of his eye. He kept it as trademark, and it seemed to have hypnotic effect on the audience. He comes on the stage this evening, as usual, dressed in black tights and wearing an enormously high and wide-brimmed topper, tall and thin as a rake. He raises his head and reveals the famous trademark. 'Good old George', yells the gallery. 'Good evening, ladies and gempmums', he solemnly replies, his deep voice rising to a falsetto on the last word. He sings us a song and plays tonight his one-string fiddle and the banjo (he has many other instruments at his command), meanwhile keeping up a nice stream of banter, ad-libs and puns with the audience, bettering anything they offer. But that isn't enough. He has left the stage as suddenly as he came but now the audience is in an uproar, 'Give us the blind boy, George'. A stranger might be puzzled. He returns with the wondering air of someone who has forgotten something; and you could hear a pin drop as he sings the tear-jerking strains of *The Blind Boy*. How he grips that audience. There is still more of the same routine.

G. H. Chirgwin portrayed by G. F. Scotson-Clark from The Halls *by George Gamble (1899)*

'The fiddler, George', is the cry. Now with a violin in his bony hands, it is *My Fiddle is my Sweetheart* .... 'And I'm her faithful beau' ....

Well, they have to let him go finally, because there is more to follow. They listen very nicely to Francisco Gaillard in a selection of new French and English songs; but you can sense that there is something else good on the way. It is a gentleman called Mr James Fawn, billed as Comedian and Singer, from The Theatre Royal, Drury Lane – a recognition of his highly successful appearances in pantomime there in recent seasons. A few years back he worked with Arthur Roberts and we are delighted to see that they will be back together later in the evening. Mr Fawn is dressed in a loud check suit and a bowler, and is a determinedly low comedian with jokes as near the knuckle as anything can get. The audience loves him dearly as he works his red-nosed way through a drunken song and a number of jokes. We take our twenty-minute interval in high good humour and order a bottle of the crusted. In the promenade on our way back from a certain noisome place, we buy a copy of *Sheard's Comic Annual for 1880*, which fortuitously contains a number of the songs that are being sung that evening.

After the interval it is left to Miss Marie Compton 'the fair gem of Serio-Comic Minstrelsy' to put us in good humour, the starters before we came to the big name of the evening, Mr Arthur Roberts, a burly figure of lugubrious appearance who, so the programme says, is an 'incomparable comedian, mimic and singer'. Dapperly dressed and highly animated once he starts, he tells some racy jokes and sings a new song called *If I was only long enough, a soldier I would be*. It is said, and we can believe it, that it was Roberts who actually invented the phrase 'near the knuckle'. You wouldn't expect a song called *I'm living with my Mother now* to be particularly suggestive; but Mr Roberts certainly makes it wildly so. When the audience has been reduced to tears, Mr Fawn comes back to join Mr Roberts in 'the screamingly funny duet' *Goodness gracious*. It is indeed screamingly funny, and leaves us in excellent mood to welcome 'the pretty little American serio-comic' Miss Ida Morris, who is making her first appearance at the Oxford that evening. The rest of the programme now moves into the traditional area of visual display, with Mlle Chelli, 'the aerial wonder and daring trapeze equilibrist'; Starelli, 'the aesthetical musical demon'; The Two Macs, 'Irish comedians and Knockabout Breakdown Artistes', who were first-rate; and Albert and Frederica, 'burlesque artistes and versatile caricaturists'. The audience becomes uncontrollably noisy during these last items, and you can see why the top people preferred to come on earlier....

So might we have spent many an enjoyable evening in the music hall through the 1890s and 1900s up to the time when, at the outbreak of the First World War, the LCC, that traditional killjoy, forbade drinking in the auditorium. The cynic may cast a doubt or two as to whether the entertainers of the 'good old days' were in any way superior to those of today. Perhaps they were not superior in technique, but they certainly knew how to handle and please a potentially riotous audience; and they could fill a theatre with their voices unaided by microphones.

The music hall was where one met these 'stars' as old friends. As they went through the circuit of the halls, in the provincial theatres as well as London, they would not need an army of script-writers to give them fresh material each week. It was not just that the old favourites would 'do' – they were *wanted*. The fame of So-and-So's new song preceded him by way of Messrs Francis & Day's 'Comic Song Annual' or some such publication, much used at the family piano. Well-tried routines were polished to the 'nth degree'. It was a rare treat to see Mr Leno or Miss Lloyd in the flesh; the instant exposure of television was not yet there to stale them.

To be top of the music-hall tree you had to be very good indeed. When Dan Leno appeared on the stage, it was as if royalty had stepped out. 'The moment he capered on', said Max Beerbohm, who was a great frequenter of the halls around the turn of the century, 'with that air of wild determination, squirming in every limb with some deep grievance

that must be outpoured, all hearts were his'. He was essentially a music-hall actor, who created his own world of characters. Great as he was in pantomime, he was not really one to live with other real characters on the stage. He was made for the music hall and gave himself completely to his audience, though the effort destroyed him. Few knew the real man, sad and melancholic, who ended by losing his reason. Well, giving oneself to the audience is the mark of a great entertainer. It was the same with Marie Lloyd, whose slightest naughty wink carried its meaning to the very back of the gallery, and was received personally by every gullible male in the house. There were many ways of achieving the same result. George Robey, who achieved the rank of 'Prime Minister of Mirth', did it by a fine show of indignation that the audience dared to laugh at him, or at any suggestion that his jokes were at all blue in tint (which of course they were). It was a fine stroke of genius to get your laughs by protesting that you were not there to be laughed at. Harry Tate vented his indignation on the small cast of idiots who accompanied his act and only made things worse when his motor-car or his golf swing went wrong. It has been said that he was the funniest man ever to step on a music-hall stage, but that claim could be made for others.

Harry Tate

There are many printed memories of the great stars of music hall. Let me insert here, with grateful acknowledgement to the author, a memory of one of those names we know but little about – Daisy Dormer. It is part of an obituary piece written by Ian Mackay in the *News Chronicle* some thirty years ago.

> She always reminded me of that lovely whimsical double star Algol, which keeps going in and out at irregular intervals, but always comes back fresh and bright and sparkling just when you think it has gone for ever. Just when you thought you had lost track of her she would turn up on Brixton Hill in a beautiful club where real fish swam round you as you danced, or in Bloomsbury, where she was the charming hostess in a cosy little tavern which she filled with Persian kittens and portraits of all the stars she had scintillated with, from Dan Leno down to the brothers Flip and Flop, who had just arrived in town. And then one grey morning she vanished again and I was sick at heart until one blessed day when I called at a wayside inn at Godalming and found my radiant goddess presiding over the provincial pint pots with all the gaiety and grace with which she had once held the whole wide world in thrall.
>
> I first fell in love with her one wild wet night in Liverpool way back in the Kaiser's war when I climbed clammily up into the 'gods' at the old Olympia to see Wilkie Bard. Mr Bard was missing for some reason, and we all booed and blew raspberries until *she* came floating on like an angel out of paradise.
>
> She came shyly from the wings, swinging her sunbonnet and looking so wistful and forlorn in the savage glare of the limes that I wanted to shout 'shame' at the big fat manager. And then she smiled at me, I'll swear, and sang *Don't You Remember California in September*, and all the bells of heaven went ringing in my ears. We cheered and cheered and clapped and clapped and she came back and gave us *The Roses Round the Door* and *Good Night, Mr Brown – I'm Out.* But it was no good. We whistled and stamped and yelled until she came back once more and sang *Back Home in Tennessee* and finally – what we had all been longing for – that immortal classic, *I Wouldn't Leave My Little Wooden Hut For You.*

The characters of music hall have not changed over the years, only the conditions and the surroundings. You could still enjoy the music-hall atmosphere at Collins' or the Met in the 1950s. You can still enjoy it in a Northern working-man's club, where many fine comics of

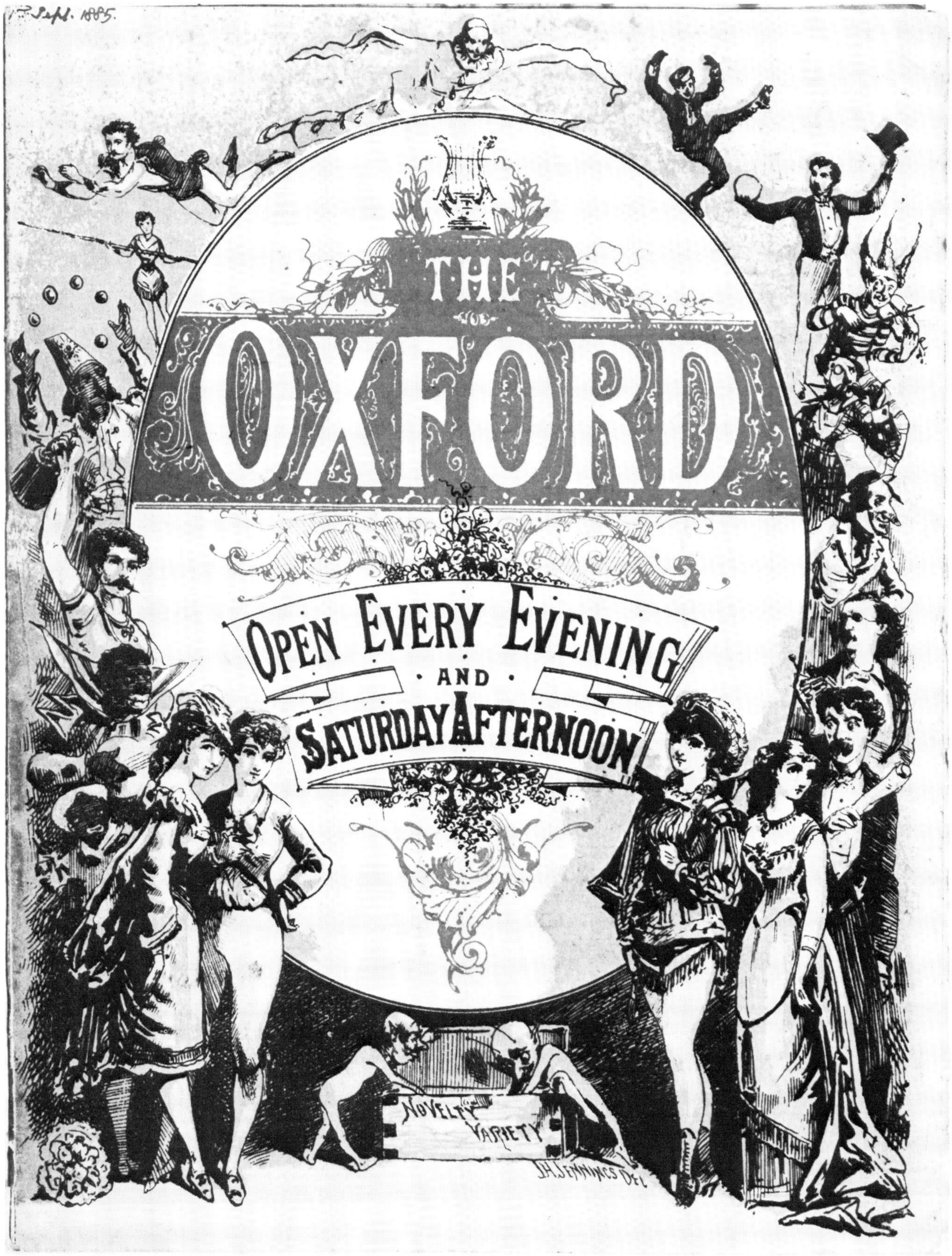
THE
OXFORD
OPEN EVERY EVENING
AND
SATURDAY AFTERNOON
NOVELTY
VARIETY
J.H. JENNINGS DEL

character, who would have been in their element in the Middlesex or the Oxford, still have to carry an audience with them and time their jokes to perfection. Even the tradition that a comic must also have a good song or two is continued, though the inevitable bit of bad crooning at the end of an otherwise satisfying act often makes us wish that it wasn't. But then these are not 'the good old days', and the songs have not got quite the earthy character that they used to have.

Many people like to slip out of the electronic age and enjoy the music hall as it was in the days of Evans's and the Canterbury. Enthusiasts for the period, and many talented artistes who understand the style, are quite capable of taking us back there in such atmospheric theatres as the Players', where Gatty's-under-the-Arches used to flourish, or in the Leeds Palace of Varieties. Under the magisterial chairmanship of Mr Leonard Sachs – who would be very much at home at Evans's (late Joy's) – and other loquacious gentlemen of the ilk, we try to slip out of our sophisticated selves and recapture the spirit of the good old days. It is not difficult, for it is everybody's privilege to dream. Perhaps if more people understood the formula we could start some good old days going again today, for the delight of future generations of reminiscers.

For obvious reasons that hardly need stating, many nostalgians would like to believe that 'the good old days' officially came to an end in 1939 or thereabouts. Such an arbitrary cut-off will look pretty silly in 2080 (if the world ever reaches such a speculative date) when, no doubt World War II will seem like only a larger-scale battle of Waterloo – after all they still used guns and bayonets and, until the very end, nice, clean, old-fashioned bombs. By now we are already aware that the Second World War years produced a reminiscent culture of their own. Even the 1950s are already a long way off to many fledgling adults.

As we have seen, the music hall was to survive as a concrete reality into the 1960s; as a type of entertainment and a spirit it is still alive and well today. In essence the age of music hall has never ended, but has subtly changed – at least the living and evolutionary music hall changed. The changes enforced by new musical fashions have altered the style of presentation and, of course, the arrival of radio and the microphone age also made a big difference. At the root of it all is the simple matter of communication and the interchange of ideas. The Atlantic became less of a divider, so that British artists and songs went over there more frequently and brought American ideas and songs back with them; and American vaudeville artistes did likewise. Till the early 1900s the traffic tended to be in the direction of America, but after that as they had more to offer, with the new strains of ragtime and jazz about to revolutionise popular music, British publishers' lists became increasingly Americanised. We have tried to echo this trend in the choice of songs in this book. We might acknowledge that the trend, in fact, started quite early – the composer of *Champagne Charlie* was an American; certainly by the 1890s there were many songs becoming familiar in the early music halls that had originated in America, such as Maude Nugent's *Sweet Rosie O'Grady*, McGlennon's *Sons of the Sea*,

Price 1/6 net.
THE DAN LENO ALBUM
CONTENTS
The Shopwalker.
The Doctor.
The Jap.
The Moving Job.
The Railway Guard.
Detective Camera.
The Recruiting Serjeant.
My Sweet Face.
Mary Ann's Refused Me.
The Midnight March.
The Waiter.
All through a little piece of Bacon.
The Grass Widower.
Her Mother's at the bottom of it all.
Nevermore.
LONDON
HERMAN DAREWSKI MUSIC PUBLISHING COMPANY, LTD. (Incorporating CHAS. SHEARD & CO.)
9-10, NEW COMPTON STREET, CHARING CROSS ROAD, W.C. 2.

followed in the 1900s by a succession of songs like *In the Good Old Summertime, Sweet Adeline* and *Put on your Old Grey bonnet.* These are songs in the old style, which could have been partly influenced by the English songs and songwriters like Harry Dacre who went to America. Of more significance were the new-style songs, with their sprightly ragtime strains – *Bill Bailey, Won't You Please Come Home* and *Wait Till The Sun Shines, Nellie* (a purely ragtime verse); and the seal put on it all by *Alexander's Ragtime Band* in 1911. The American Ragtime Octette came over in the 1900s and deposited Nat D. Ayer on our doorsteps. Then came the Original Dixieland Jazz Band to set the jazz flame alight – and George Robey indignantly refused to appear on the same bill with them. If there is not much jazz evident in these pages, it is because the music hall proper tended to conservatism. Music hall in its new and brasher forms began to use the new jazz songs like *I'm just wild about Harry* in the 1920s.

If radio and television helped the cinema gradually to stifle live music hall, they also did their level best to promote it. The variety show was very much a part of the radio scene. The difference was, however, that when we went to a seaside variety show in the 1930s we were really going to see in the flesh people whose voices we had often heard through disembodied radio waves. Nobody would deny that there was plenty of music-hall talent around – Max Miller, George Formby Jr, Nellie Wallace, Gracie Fields, The Crazy Gang, Will Hay, Robb Wilton, the Western Brothers, Florence Desmond – the faint difference was the sort of legendary aura that radio gave them; a step on the way to the remoteness of cinema and TV stars. They were glossier and very highly paid and had long ceased to be ordinary people entertaining their friends. Break down the barriers, of course, and it becomes a false image. Meet somebody like Tommy Trinder and you are meeting a true music-hall character, spontaneous and witty, an entertainer, a human personality in no need of script-writers or producers – simply an audience.

So in essence it is not music hall that has died but the music halls. Today the last provincial palaces of variety are disappearing. In the thirties many of them became cinemas; now the cinemas themselves become bingo halls. A few façades remain to remind us of the warm-hearted evenings that once went on within. Those were the good old days. . . .

Further Reading

The literature of music hall is itself of considerable interest, most of it offering insight into what made the good old days tick along. The first brief volume on the subject was probably the moralising *Music Hall, As It Is, As It Might Have Been* (Smart & Allen, 1880) by 'A. Spectator'; the second was *Music Hall Land* (Ward & Downey, 1890) by Percy Fitzgerald, a random account of the entertainers and 'General Oddities of that Strange Country'. The first full-length survey of music hall was *The Variety Stage* (T. Fisher Unwin, 1895) by Charles Douglas Stuart, proprietor and editor of various early music-hall magazines, and A. J. Park: an out-of-print volume, but packed full of practical details of the variety world, which have been a constant source of information for later writers. While some of the eye-witness facts are invaluable, there are some inaccuracies which have to be double-checked. There appears to have been no other book entirely devoted to the history of the music hall until *Idols of the Halls* by H. Chance Newton (Heath Cranton, 1928) appeared. This again was valuable for memories of personal experience and acquaintanceship, recounted by a well-known music critic of the day. *The Story of the Music Hall* (Fleetway, 1935) by Archibald Haddon was a large, rambling book with little sense of order but full of personal insight, by a creditable journalist. *Winkles and Champagne* (Batsford, 1938) by M. Willson Disher, although not entirely devoted to music hall, was the first book to realise fully the romantic associations of the art, its music-covers and associated items, looked at in perspective in a beautifully produced volume. The same author provided a potted version in a popular series in *Fairs, Circuses and Music Halls* (Collins, 1942). *Stars Who Made the Halls* (T. Werner Laurie, 1946) by S. Theodore Felstead was a book of first-hand impressions of music-hall entertainers. The best academically written history to date is *The Early Doors* (Nicholson & Watson, 1946) by Harold Scott, a revivalist music-hall chairman, and it remains *the* classic volume on the subject. *The Melodies Linger On* (W. H. Allen, 1951) was a typical W. Macqueen Pope production, richly emotional and nostalgic, a comprehensive work but sadly lacking in dates. These might be considered the pioneering works on the subject.

The more recent general interest in the subject was heralded by *British Music Hall* (Studio Vista, 1965; revised & enlarged edition, Gentry, 1974) a valuable collection of illustrative material from the archives of Raymond Mander and Joe Mitchenson and elsewhere, accompanied by a brief but very detailed history and caption comments. *Sweet Saturday Night* (MacGibbon & Kee, 1967) by Colin MacInnes was an affectionately nostalgic book full of interesting insights. With so much emphasis on the London music hall, it was good to look at its other spheres of activity in a thoroughly researched book,

The Northern Music Hall (Graham, 1970), by G. J. Mellor; and an Irish viewpoint in *Infinite Variety: Dan Lowry's Music-Hall 1879–97* (Gill & Macmillan, 1975) by Eugene Watters. A valuable documentary on the music hall which gave much insight into the finances and organisation of music halls, as well as the history of its rise, establishment and decline, was *Music Hall in Britain* (David & Charles, 1975) by D. F. Cheshire.

Dictionaries or encyclopaedias of music hall face the problem that so much information is missing or lost. *'The Performer' Who's Who in Variety* (The Performer, 1950) by G. R. Bullar and Len Evans tried to provide a practical guide but confined itself to performers still active. Building on the foundation of this book and adding more about the past artistes comes *British Music Hall: an Illustrated Who's Who from 1850 to the Present Day* (Elek, 1976) by Roy Busby, an invaluable book only

Music Hall Proprietor, from Mr Punch's Model Music-Hall *by F. Anstey (1892)*

limited by what is no longer available. An early guide for the profession was *The London Music Hall Artiste's Vade Mecum or Constant Companion* by Brandon Phillips (Sinclair, 1899). The first move toward a definitive discography of the subject came with *British Music Hall on Record* by Brian Rust (Gramophone Publications, 1979).

Various shorter books concerning the performers have appeared through the years: *The Halls* (Fisher Unwin, 1899) had a brief text by George Gamble and lively drawings by G. F. Scotson-Clark. There were also *Music Hall Memories* (Selwyn & Blount, 1927) edited by Terence Prentis; *Old-Time Music Hall Comedians* (privately printed, 1949) by Sir Louis Fergusson; *Music Hall Stars of the Nineties* (British Technical & General Press, 1952) by George Le Roy; and in more recent time *Your Own, Your Very Own* (Allan, 1971) by Peter Gammond, and *Music Hall* (Eyre – Methuen, 1976) by Roy Hudd, illustrated scrapbooks by two music-hall collectors. Of associated interest was a book of *Punch* parodies, *Mr Punch's Model Music-Hall Songs and Dramas* (Bradbury Agnew, 1892) by F. Anstey; and a romanticised study of the music-hall atmosphere and its stars, *Music Hall Nights* (Lane, 1925) by Dion Clayton Calthrop.

Eugene Stratton

Concentrating on the music and songs of the music hall came a pioneering book, *They Were Singing* (Harrap, 1952), by Christopher Pulling; and some music-hall ground was covered in *Victorian Song: from Dive to Drawing Room* (Phoenix House, 1955) by M. Willson Disher, and *Seven Centuries of Popular Song* (Phoenix House, 1956) by Reginald Nettel. There have been some useful collections of songs with accompanying text in recent years, including *Songs of the British Music Hall* (Oak, New York, 1971) by Peter Davison; *Music Hall Song Book* (David & Charles/EMI, 1975), a predecessor of the present book drawing on the Francis, Day & Hunter & Feldman catalogues, edited by Peter Gammond; *Sixty Years of British Music Hall* (Chappell/Deutsch, 1976), drawing on the Ascherberg, Hopwood & Crew lists, edited by John M. Garrett. Some early material was to be found in *An English Song Book* (Chapman & Hall, 1925) edited by Harold Scott; some of the song-and-supper material in *Bawdy Songs of the Early Music-Hall* (David & Charles, 1975) edited by George Speaight; and *Victorian Folk Songs* (Essex, 1965) edited by Charles Chilton. A lowbrow lyrical comment on life in the early twentieth century is to be found in *Best Music Hall & Variety Songs* (Wolfe, 1972).

The halls themselves were first discussed in *Theatres and Music Halls* by Stewart D. Headlam (Women's Printing Society, 1877), followed by *Old Music Halls* (a *John o' London's* supplement, 1924) by Sir Richard Terry. The authoritative book giving facts and figures from official records is *London Theatres and Music Halls* (Library Association, 1970) by Diana Howard. The subject is covered in many of the music-hall histories as well. The modern Players' Theatre has its own literature: *Late Joys at the Players' Theatre* (Boardman, 1943) edited by Jean Anderson; *Players' Joys* (Players' Theatre, 1962) edited by Hal D. Stewart; and *Late and Early Joys at the Players' Theatre* (Boardman, 1952) edited by Paul Sheridan.

Sidelights and comments on music hall, sketches of its performers and the general background naturally appear in a variety of books of which the following are worth noting: *Immoment Toys* (Cape, 1945) by James Agate, containing a number of 'profiles'; various volumes of essays and reviews by Max Beerbohm – *More* (1899), *Mainly on the Air* (1946), *Around Theatres* (1953), *More Theatres* (1969), *Last Theatres* (1970); *Bow Bell Memories* (not dated) by Louis Bamberger; various discursive volumes by the sporting journalist J. B. Booth – *Old Pink 'Un Days* (1924), *Masters and Men* (1926), *London Town* (1929), *Pink Parade* (1933), *A Pink 'Un Remembers* (1937), *The Days We Knew* (1943) and *Seventy Years of Song* (1943) which he edited; W. Buchanan-Taylor in *Shake the Bottle* (1942), *Shake It Again* (1943) and *One More Shake* (1944); *London in My Time* (1934) by Thomas Burke; *The Joy of the Theatre* (1913) by Gilbert Cannan; *Full Score* (1970) by Sir Neville Cardus; *Crowded Nights and Days* (1930) by Arthur Croxton; *London Nights of Long Ago* (1927) by Shaw Desmond; *Selected Essays 1917–1932* (1932, and later collections) by T. S. Eliot; by Jimmy Glover – *Jimmy Glover – His Book* (1911), *Jimmy Glover and his Friends* (1913), *Hims Ancient and Modern* (1926); *My Melodious Memories* (1937) by Herman Finck; *Fifty Years of a Londoner's Life* (1916) & *A Playgoer's Memories* (1920) by H. G. Hibbert; *Music of the People* (1970) by Edward Lee; *Popular Entertainment Through the Ages* (1932) by Samuel McKechnie; *Night Life* (1926) by Ralph Nevill; *Swings and Roundabouts* (1919) by T. McDonald Rendle; *Ring Up the Curtain* (1938) by Ernest Short and Arthur Compton-Rickett; *Fifty Years of Vaudeville* (1946) by Ernest Short; *From Theatre to Music Hall* (1912), *London Scenes* (1920), and *A Candle to the Stars* (1932) by W. R. Titterton; *101 Jubilee Road* (1948) by Frederick Willis; *East End Entertainment* (1954) by A. E. Wilson; and *Nights in London* (1926) by Horace Wyndham. Going back to Song-and-Supper Days, references are to be found in *Green-Room Recollections* (1896) by Arthur William A'Beckett; *Mister Pips – His Diary* (1849) by Spencer Leigh; *London in the Sixties* (1909) by 'One of the Old Brigade'; *The Night Side of London* (1858) by J. Ewing Ritchie; *Recollections and Experiences* (1884) and other books by Edmund Yates.

Of autobiographies and biographies concerning music hall and variety figures there are a number to mention, including (in alphabetical order): *Footlight Memories* (not dated) by George W. Alltree; *Vaudeville Days* (1935) by W. H. Boardman; *Albert Chevalier* (1896) by Albert Chevalier and Brian Daly; *Before I Forget* (1901) by Albert Chevalier; *Chirgwin's Chirrup: Life and Reminiscences* (1912) by G. H. Chirgwin; *The Man Who Broke the Bank* (1930) by Charles Coborn; *The Cowells in America* (1934) by M. Willson Disher; *The Autobiography of an Eccentric Comedian* (not dated) by T. E. Dunville; *Sing As We Go* (1960) by Gracie Fields; *Clowning Through* (1927) by Frank Foster; *The Spice of Life* (1939) by George Foster; *Vagaries of a Vagabond* (1930) by George Gray; *A Modern Columbus* (1918) by R. G. Knowles; by Harry Lauder – *At Home and on Tour* (1912), *A Minstrel in France* (1918), *Roamin' in the Gloamin'* (1927) and *Wee Drappies* (1931);

Dan Leno at home

Great Scot (Harry Lauder) (1968) by Gordon Irving; *Working the Halls* (1973) by Peter Honri; *Hys Booke* (1901; abridged edition, 1968) by Dan Leno; *Dan Leno* (1905) by J. Hickory Wood; *The Funniest Man on Earth: The Story of Dan Leno* (1977) by Gyles Brandreth; *Our Marie (Marie Lloyd)* (1936) by Naomi Jacob; *Marie Lloyd, Queen of the Music-Halls* (not dated) by W. Macqueen Pope; *Marie Lloyd and Music Hall* (1972) by Daniel Farson (much of general nature as well); *Fixing the Stoof Oop* (not dated) by Billy Merson; *Sixty Years' Stage Service (Charles Morton)* (1905) by W. H. Morton & H. Chance Newton; *Limelight* (1938) by George Mozart; *Stories and Anecdotes* (not dated) & *The Merriest Man Alive* (not dated) by Jolly John Nash; *Harry Randall, Old Time Comedian* (not dated) by Harry Randall; *Take It For a Fact* (1954) by Ada Reeve; *A Book of Travels (and Wanderings)* (1911) by Harry Relph (Little Tich); *The Adventures of Arthur Roberts* (1898) and *Fifty Years of Spoof* (1927) by Arthur Roberts; *My Life Up to Now* (1908) by George Robey; *Looking Back on Life* (1933) by George Robey; *Prime Minister of Mirth (George Robey)* (1956) by A. E. Wilson; *George Robey* (1972) by Peter Cotes; *Red Plush and Greasepaint* (1964) by Clarkson Rose; *Recollections of Vesta Tilley* (1934) by Lady de Frece (Vesta Tilley); *Reminiscences of J. L. Toole* (1889) by Joseph Hatton; *I Had to Be 'Wee'* (1948) by Georgie Wood; as supplement to these, *Funny Way to be a Hero* (1973) by John Fisher adds profiles of many later comedians connected with the halls.

As we have dealt entirely with British music hall, there is only

need of a brief mention of a couple of books that set the equivalent American scene—*American Vaudeville* (1940) by Douglas Gilbert; and *Vaudeville* (1953) by Joe Laurie. The French music hall (as well as British) is accessibly covered in *Cent Ans de Music-Hall* (1956) by Jacques-Charles. The most international survey to appear so far is *A Hard Act to Follow* (1978) by Peter Leslie.

In addition to the song-books (with text) mentioned above, collectors should be reminded of the standard *60 Old-Time Variety Songs*, which started life in the 1930s as the *News Chronicle Song Book No 2* (with introduction by Charles Coborn & appreciation by George Robey) has since been reprinted several times and recently came out in a smart new edition: EMI Music Publishing Ltd, 1977. The titles included are: *After the Ball; Ask a Policeman; At my Time of Life; At Trinity Church; The Banshee; The Blind Boy; A Broken Doll; Coal Black Mammy; Comrades; Daddy Wouldn't Buy Me a Bow-wow; Daisy Bell; Down the Road; Flanagan; Following in Father's Footsteps; Fol the rol-lol; For Old Time's Sake; The Galloping Major; The Honeysuckle and the Bee; I Love a Lassie; I Married a Wife; I Want to Sing in Opera; I Wouldn't Leave My Little Wooden Hut for You; If it Wasn't For the 'Ouses in between; If those Lips Could Only Speak; I'll Take You Home Again, Kathleen; I'm Henery the Eighth; In the Shade of the Old Apple Tree; In the Twi-twi-twilight; In these Hard Times; It's a Great Big Shame; It's Nice to Get up in the Morning; Joshua; Just Like the Ivy; Let's All Go Down the Strand; The Lily of Laguna; A Little Bit Off the Top; Little Dolly Daydream; The Man Who Broke the Bank at Monte Carlo; The Miner's Dream of Home; My Fiddle Is My Sweetheart; The Mystery of a Hansom Cab; The Old Rustic Bridge by the Mill; Piccadilly Johnny; Put on Your Tat-ta, Little Girlie; In the Shade of the Palm; She Was One of the Early Birds; Silver Threads among the Gold; Sister Mary Walked Like That; Skylark; Soldiers of the Queen; Swanee; Ting, Ting, That's How the Bell Goes; Twiggy Voo; Two Little Girls in Blue; Two Lovely Black Eyes; Waiting for the Robert E. Lee; What ho, She Bumps; When You're All Dressed up; Where Did You Get that Hat; You Made me Love You. Music Hall Songbook* (EMI Music Publishing/David & Charles), with 45 songs, included some of these and also *A Bird in a Gilded Cage; Come, Josephine, in my Flying Machine; Don't Dilly Dally on the Way; Down at the old Bull and Bush; Goodbye, Dolly Gray; Hello, Hello, Who's Your Lady Friend; Her Golden Hair was Hanging Down Her Back; I Do Like to be beside the Seaside; I Live in Trafalgar Square; I'm shy, Mary Ellen; If I Should Plant a Tiny Seed of Love; If You Were the Only Girl in the World; It's a Long Way to Tipperary; Jolly Good Luck to the Girl Who Loves a Soldier; A Little of What you Fancy Does You Good; Lucky Jim; My Old Dutch; Oh, You Beautiful Doll; On the Good Ship Yacki-Hicki-Doola; Poor John; Roamin' in the Gloamin'; She Sells Seashells; Ship ahoy; The Spaniard that Blighted My Life; Swing me Higher, Obadiah; Ta-ra-ra-boom-de-ay; Waiting at The Church; When Father Papered the Parlour* and *Wot Cher!* None of the above titles (apart from *The old Bull and Bush*) are included in the present collection.

Vilikins And His Dinah

Arranged by
AUBREY KENNETT.

4

Then go, boldest daughter, her parient replied,
As you won't agree to be this here young man's bride,
I shall leave your large fortune to the nearest of kin,
And you shan't have the benefit of one single pin.
Singing *etc.*

5

As Vil-i-kins was a val-i-king the garden one day,
He spied his own Dinah lying dead upon the way,
And a cup of cold pi-son, it stood by her side,
With a billet-dux as stated that by pi-son she died.
Singing *etc.*

6

He kissed her cold corpus a thousand times o'er,
To be parted from Dinah he could not endure,
So he drank up the pi-son like a true lov-yer brave,
And Vilikins and his Dinah were buried in one grave.
Singing *etc.*

Moral

Now all nice young maidens take warning! be sure—
Never not by no means offend the guv'nor,
And all gay young batchelors mind who you set eyes on,
Think of Vilikins and Dinah and the cup of cold pi-son.
Singing *etc.*

The Mermaid

Words by THACKERAY

Music by ALFRED LEE

2. Surpris'd will be my com-ri-ades,
 And the friends I've got left on the shore
 And my poor grandmother, whom, alas!
 I never shall see more,
 When she hears as I've been summoned
 Away quite suddenlee,
 To be mar-ri-ed to a mer-mi-ade,
 At the bottom of the deep blue sea,
 Chorus. Singing, Rule Britannia, *etc.*

3. There's a brocken sixpence in my purse,
 Likewise a lock of hair,
 To Sally I solicitize,
 As you will safely bear;
 And you will say unto her,
 It was bare necessitee
 That made me wed this here mer-mi-ade,
 At the bottom of the deep blue sea,
 Chorus. Singing, Rule Britannia, *etc.*

4. 'Tis true, that to refresh myself,
 No baccy now I gets,
 But, then, as with respects to that,
 Myself I never frets,
 For all the joys of life are
 Immaterial to me
 Now I'm mar-ri-ed to a mer-mi-ade,
 At the bottom of the deep blue sea,
 Chorus. Singing, Rule Britannia, *etc.*

5. When I see'd and heer'd this here drownded man,
 My limbs with terror shook,
 I ax'ed him qui-es-ti-ons,
 For the words my lips forsook;
 And then straightways he swoonded,
 And said no more unto me,
 But dived down to his mer-mi-ade,
 At the bottom of the deep blue sea.
 Chorus. Singing, Rule Britannia, *etc.*

Champagne Charlie

Original Lyrics by
GEORGE LEYBOURNE
Revised Lyrics by
ERNEST IRVING & FRANK EYTON

Music by
ALFRED LEE

CHORUS

Cham-pagne Char-lie is my name, Cham-pagne drink-ing is my game,
p-f
C
There's no drink as good as fizz! fizz! fizz! I'll drink ev-'ry drop there is, is, is!
Cdim Dm7 G7 C#dim G7
All round town it is the same, By Pop! Pop! Pop! I rose to fame,
C
1 2
I'm the I-dol of the bar-maids, And Champagne Charlie is my name. name.
Am D7-♭5 C G7 Gdim G7 C G7 C G7 C
D.C.

The Man On The Flying Trapeze

Words by
GEORGE LEYBOURNE

Music by
ALFRED LEE.

hand - some, ... I tried all I knew, her to please, ... But
peo - ple be - low, And one night he smil'd on my love, ... She
there ev - 'ry night And would throw him Bou - quets on the stage, ... Which
- loped in the night With him, with the great - est of ease, ... From
dress'd her in tights, To help him to live at his ease, ... And
Fmi C7 Fmi C7
I could not please her one quarter so well, Like that man up - on the Tra - peze.
wink'd back at him and she shout - ed "Bra - vo!" As he hung by his nose up a - bove.
caused him to meet her, how he ran me down, To tell you would take a whole page
two sto - reys high, he had low - er'd her down To the ground on his fly - ing Tra - peze!
made her as - sume...... a mas - cu - line name, And now she goes on the Tra - peze!
Fmi C7 Fmi C7 Fmi Db7 C7 Fmi
CHORUS
Whoa! He'd fly thro' the air with the greatest of ease, A dar - ing young man on the fly - ing Tra -
Last Chos. Whoa! She floats thro' the air with the greatest of ease, You'd think her a man on the fly - ing Tra -
mf
Eb7 Ab F7 Bb7 Eb7 Ab Abaug
- peze, His movements were graceful, All girls he could please, And my love he's {purloin'd stolen} a - way. ....
- peze, She does all the work.... While he takes his ease, And that's what become of my love. ....
Ab Ab7 F7 Bb7 Dbmi Eb7 dim Eb7 Ab Bb7 Eb7 Ab Eb Ab D.C.

Oh, The Fairies

Words by
T. S. LONSDALE

Music by
W. G. EATON

you come with me, You'll be in for the diz - zi - est time"........... In - side thea - tre
heart gave a thump And his sen - ses went all ting - a - ling............. Oh! yes, you are
D A7 D A7
walls, He lounged in the stalls, And he sat thro' a grand pan - to - mine......................
right, He's there ev - 'ry night, In the day - time you can hear him sing:......................
rall.
D Ddim D A7 Adim A7 D Gm Ddim D7
CHORUS
Oh, the fai - ries, whoa, the fai - ries, Nothing but splendour and fem-in-ine gen - der......
p–f a tempo
G C D7 G C G A7 D7 D+
1 2
Oh, the fai - ries, whoa, the fai - ries, Oh, for a wing of a fai - ry queen. queen.
f
D.C.
G C D Em Gdim G C G A7 (♭5) D7 G D7 G

He's Going To Marry Mary Ann

Written and Composed by JOSEPH TABRAR.

Oh, shout hooray for Ma-ry Ann! I'm go-ing to get wed To-
F C7/F F A D D♭° F
-morrow af-ter-noon at one To my young fellow, Fred. He's
G7 C G C
saved up in the Saving's Bank Six pounds or there-a-bout, This
C7 F Fm F F A
ve-ry day, to buy the home, He drew the mo-ney out:—
E♭° D7 Gm G7(♭5) F C7 F

CHORUS.

He's bought a bed, and a ta-ble too, A big tin dish for making stew, A large flat-iron to
F D7 Gm E7 Am
iron his shirt, And a flannel, and a scrubbing-brush to wash away the dirt. And he's bought a pail, and
F7 Gm D♭° C7 F
basins three, A coffee-pot, a kettle, and a tea-pot for the tea, And a soap-bowl, and a ladle, And a
D7 Gm E7 (♭5) E♭°
gridiron, and a cradle, And he's going to mar-ry Ma-ry Ann— that's me! He's
Gm D♭° F C7 F
going to marry Ma-ry Ann!
F C7 F D7 Gm C7 F

1.

Oh, shout hooray for Mary Ann!
I'm going to get wed
To-morrow afternoon at one,
To my young fellow, Fred.
He's saved up in the Savings Bank
Six pounds or thereabout,
This very day, to buy the home,
He drew the money out:—

CHORUS.

He's bought a bed, and a table too,
A big tin dish for making stew,
A large flat-iron, to iron his shirt,
And a flannel, and a scrubbing brush to wash away the dirt.
And he's bought a pail and basins three,
A coffee-pot, a kettle, and a tea-pot for the tea,
And a soap-bowl and a ladle,
And a gridiron, and a cradle,
And he's going to marry Mary Ann— that's *me!*
He's going to marry Mary Ann!

2.

My friends remark: "Oh, what a lark
To see the money fly!"
They say we're two young sillies, and
We don't know what to buy.
But you just leave my Fred alone,
He's such a knowing sort,
He lays the money out A. 1.
And this is what he's bought:—
(Chorus.)— He's bought a bed, &c.

3.

He went right off to Maple's, where
The furniture is grand,
He said he meant to have things new,
Not common second-hand.
We've got one chair, one table, and
One chest of drawers, two mugs,
Two plates, two cups, two saucers, and
A pair of water-jugs:—
(Chorus.)— He's bought a bed, &c.

He's All Right When You Know Him

Words and Music by
CHARLES COBORN

Spoken after 1st Verse:-

'Ere, you know *Bill*. He's right enough, ain't he? Well—

(*Chorus*)

Spoken after 2nd Verse:-

'Ere, you know *Bill*. He can shift it, can't he? I tell yer—

(*Chorus*)

Spoken after 3rd Verse:-

I tell yer, you don't half know what the man can do!—

(*Chorus*)

Spoken after 4th Verse:-

But that's what I blame Bill for, roundin' on them bobbies. What I says, Coppers is werry pretty things and they take a lot of keeping up, but they're like everythink else, they won't last if yer knock 'em about—

(*Chorus*)

CHORUS

He's all right when you know him though he's has - ty when he's wex'd, He'll
mp f
G D7 G D G
black your eye one min-ute, and he'll stand a pint the next. He would-n't hurt a ba - by, he's a
D7 G A7 D D7 G
pal as you can trust, He's all right when you know him, but you've
A7 D7 G D7 G
1 2
got to know him fust. He's got to know him fust.
D7 G D7 G E7 D7 G D7

Young Men Taken In And Done For

Arranged by
GEORGE LE BRUNN

Written & Composed by
HARRY KING.

Lu - cy Jaggs, she knock'd me out of time; I call'd there for a -
mo - ther then soon show'd me what she had; I'd not stay'd there a -
hap - . pi - ness but that's all "tom - my rot!" I don't be - lieve my
Em A7 D A
- part - ments, for I'd no tic'd once or twice, A
bove a week when Lu - cy came to me, And
wife loves me, it's the truth I'm tell - ing you, A
B7 E7 A
card stuck in the win - dow, and......... on it this de - vice;
fond - ly kiss'd me on my cheek, then sat me on her knee!
wife can't love her hus-band much if she beats him black and blue.
Bm Adim A E7 A

CHORUS *Tempo di marcia*

The Lowther Arcade

(THE TIN GEE GEE)

Revised by
MEL. B. SPURR.

Written & Composed by
FRED CAPE.

you can pur - chase a dol - ly or a spade For your
G
C
Am7
good lit - tle girls and boys. And ......
D7
G
as I pass'd a cer - tain stall Said a
D
G
Em
a tempo
lit - tle wee voice to me: — "Oh,
rit
A
D

I am a colo - nel in a lit - tle cock'd hat, And I
G
C
Am7
ride on a tin gee - gee: Oh, ...
D7
G
I am a colo - nel in a lit - tle cock'd hat And I
G
C6
Am7
ride on a tin gee - - gee."
D
G

THE LOWTHER ARCADE.

Written and Composed by FRED CAPE. Revised and Sung by MEL. B. SPURR.

I was strolling, one day, down the Lowther Arcade,
That place for children's toys,
Where you may purchase a dolly or a spade,
For your good little girls and boys.
And, as I passed a certain stall, said a little wee voice to me:
(*Bis.*) "Oh, I am a Colonel in a little cocked hat, and I ride on a tin gee-gee."

Then I looked, and a little tin soldier I saw,
In his little cocked hat, so fine
He'd a little tin sword that shone in the light,
As he led a glittering line
Of tin hussars whose sabres flashed, in a manner à la militaree.
(*Bis.*) Whilst that little tin soldier he rode at their head, so proud, on his tin gee-gee.

3.

Then that little tin soldier, he sobbed and he sighed,
So I patted his little tin head:
"What vexes your little tin soul?" said I,
And this is what he said:
"I've been on this stall a very long time, and I'm marked one-and-nine, as you see,
(*Bis.*) While just on the shelf above my head, there's a fellow marked two-and-three!

4.

"Now, he hasn't got a sword and he hasn't got a horse,
And I'm quite as good as he:
Then why mark me at one-and-nine,
And him at two-and-three?
There's a pretty little dolly-girl, over there, and I'm madly in love with she,
{But now that I'm only marked one-and-nine, she turns up her nose at me:
{She turns up her little wax nose at me, and flirts with two-and-three.

5.

"And, oh! she's dressed in a beautiful dress,
It's a dress I do admire:
She has pearly blue eyes, that open and shut,
When worked inside by a wire.
And, once on a time, when the folks had gone, she used to ogle *me*:
{But now that I'm only marked one-and-nine, she turns up her nose at me:
{She turns up her little *snub* nose at me, and *carries on* with two-and-three."

6.

"Cheer up, my little tin man," said I,
"I'll see what I can do:
You're a fine little fellow, and it is a shame
That she should so treat you."
So I took down the label from the upper shelf, and I labelled him two-and-three,
{And I marked the other one one-and-nine, which was very, very wrong of me,
{But I felt so sorry for that little tin soul, as he rode on his tin gee-gee.

7

Now, that little tin soldier he puffed with pride,
At being mark'd two-and-three.
And that saucy little dolly-girl smiled, once more,
For he'd risen in life, do you see?
And it's so in this world, for I'm in love with a maiden of high degree,
{But I am only marked one-and-nine, and the other chap's two-and three:
{And a girl never looks at one-and-nine, with a possible two-and-three!

The Future Mrs. 'Awkins

by ALBERT CHEVALIER

me. At first she said she would-n't, then she said she could-n't
Bb7
Then she whis - pered "Well, I'll see" Sez
Eb
I "be Mis - sis 'Aw - kins, Mis - sis 'En - 'ry 'Aw - kins,
Ab
Eb
Or a - crost the seas I'll roam. So
Bb7
Eb

'elp me bob I'm cra - zy, Li - zer you're a dai - sy.
Ab
Eb
Won't you share my 'um - ble 'ome? *Won't yer?* Oh! Li - zer!
colla voce.
F7
Eb
Abm6
Sweet Li - zer! If yer die an old maid you'll 'ave
Eb
Abm6
Eb
on - ly yer - self to blame D'y'ear Li - zer? Dear Li - zer!
F7
Bb7
Eb
Abm
Eb
Abm

2. I shan't forgit our meetin', "G'arn," was'er greetin'
"Just yer mind wot you're about;"
'Er pretty 'ead she throws up, then she turns 'er nose up,
Sayin' "let me go I'll shout!"
"I like your style," sez Lizer, thought as I'd surprise 'er
Cops 'er round the waist like this!
Sez she "I must be dreamin', chuck it I'll start screamin' "
"If yer do" sez I "I'll kiss."
(Spoken or Sung:) "Now then"
Oh! Lizer! Sweet Lizer!
If yer die an old maid you'll 'ave only yerself to blame!
D'y'ear Lizer. Dear Lizer!
'Ow d'yer fancy 'Awkins for your other name?

3. She wears a artful bonnit feathers stuck upon it,
Coverin' a fringe all curled;
She's just about the sweetest, prettiest and neatest
Doner in the wide, wide world!
And she'll be Mrs. 'Awkins, Mrs. 'En'ry 'Awkins
Got'er for to name the day;
Settled it last Monday so to church on Sunday
Off we trots the donkey shay!
(Spoken or Sung:) "Now then"
Oh! Lizer! Sweet Lizer!
If yer died an old maid you'd 'ave only yerself to blame
D'y'ear Lizer? Dear Lizer!
Mrs. 'En'ry Awkins is a first class name!

Sweet Rosie O'Grady

Words and Music by MAUDE NUGENT.

Tempo di Valse

CHORUS

Sons Of The Sea

Written and Composed by FELIX Mc GLENNON

-get, they for-get; The lads in blue they've met, Oft - en met, oft - en met.
-get, they for-get; The lads in blue they've met, Oft - en met, oft - en met.
-get, they for-get; The lads in blue they've met, Oft - en met, oft - en met.
C#7 F#m C# F#m C#7 F#m C#7 F#m C#
CHORUS Tempo di Marcia
Sons of the sea! All Brit-ish born! Sail - ing ev - 'ry
p 2nd ff
cresc.
A E7 F#7
o - cean, Laugh-ing foes to scorn. They may build their ships, my lads, and
mf
Bm E7 A
think they know the game, But they can't build boys of the bull-dog breed, Who made old Eng-land's
accel. cres - cen - do
E7 F° Bm E7
1 2
D. 𝄋
name! name!
ff f cresc.
A Bm7 E A A Bm A E7 A

Our Lodger's Such A Nice Young Man

Words and Music by
FRED MURRAY and
LAURENCE BARCLAY

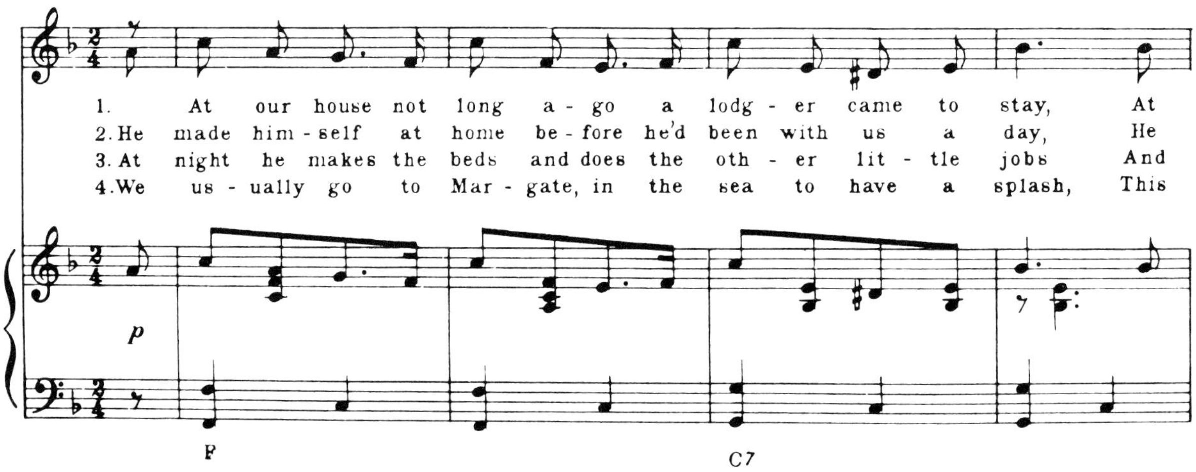

first I felt as if I'd like to drive him right a - way; But
kissed mam - ma and all of us, 'cos pa - pa was a - way; Be -
if the ba - by hurts it - self he real - ly cries and sobs; On
year Pa said, "I'm bus - y!" but I think he had no cash; The
F
soon he proved him - self to be so ve - ry good and kind, That,
- fore he goes to work he lights the fires and scrubs the floor, And
Sun - day when ma's cook - ing and pa - pa is at the club, He
lodg - er took us down in - stead, mam - ma and ba - by too, And
A7
Dm
Gm
Dm
like my dear mam - ma, I quite made up my lit - tle mind.
puts a nice strong cup of tea out - side ma's bed - room door.
takes the kids and baths us all in - side the wash - ing tub.
nev - er charged Pa an - y - thing - now there's a pal for you!
G7
C
CO
C7

CHORUS

Our__ lodg - er's such a nice young man, such a good young man is he;
mf-f
F Dm A7 Dm
So__ good, so__ kind, to all our fam - i - ly! He's__ nev - er going to
G7 F Dm7 G7 C7 F
leave us- Oh dear, oh dear no! He's such a good,
Dm A7 Dm A Dm F C7
good - y, good - y man, mam - ma told me so. so.__
Gm C7 F F○ F F○ F C7 F 8
D.C.

I'll Be Your Sweetheart

Words and Music by
HARRY DACRE

so I stood and watched the youth-ful pair The lad all blush-ing gave the maid a
I should nev-er be your dar-ling wife He shook his head and took an-oth-er
hap-pi-est young cou-ple in the land And once a-gain he took the lov-ing
G7 Gm7 C7 Gm7 C7
kiss Then ten-der-ly he whis-pered this
kiss Then once a-gain he whis-pered this
kiss Then pas-sion-ate-ly whis-pered this
F G7 Dm7 G9 Gm7 C7
I'll be your sweet-heart if
F F Ab° C7 Gm7
(A Bass)
you will be mine All my
C7 F Db7 Gm7 C7 F Am
(A Bass) (Ab Bass) (E Bass)

life I'll be your val - len - tine
Eb° D7 Gm9 C7
Blue - bells I've gath - ered keep them and be
F F Ab° C7 Gm7 C7
(A Bass)
true When I'm a man my plan
F Db7 Gm7 C7 F A7 F7 Bb Gm Bb
(A Bass) (Ab Bass) (G Bass) (A Bass)
1
2
will be to mar - ry you. you.
D.%
C7 F Db7 Gm7 C7 F
(A Bass) (Ab Bass)

Hello! Ma Baby

Written and Composed by
HOWARD and EMERSON

Medium tempo

nev - er seen ma hon - ey, but she's mine, all right, So take my tip, and leave this gal a -
sat - is-fied be-cause I'se got ma babe's ad - dress, Here past - ed in the lin - ing of ma
Fm7
Bb7
Fm7
Bb7
-lone. Ev - 'ry sin - gle morn - ing you will hear me yell, "Hey,
hat. I am might - y scared,'cause if the wires get crossed, 'Twill
Eb
F9
Bb13
Eb
Eb+
Eb6
Eb
Cen - tral! fix me up a - long the line." She con - nects me with ma hon - ey, then she
sep - ar - ate from me ma ba - by mine; Then some oth - er coon will win her, and ma
C7
Fm
C7
Fm
Ab
Cdim
rings the bell, And this is what I say to ba - by mine.
game is lost, And so each day I shout a - long the line.
Eb
G7(5b)
C7
Cm7
F7
Bb
dim
Bb7

CHORUS Medium tempo

Burlington Bertie

Words and Music by HARRY B. NORRIS.

brooch or a new dia - mond ring. And thinks a seal jack - et is
turns up, the lone - ly girl's friend? Who is it that night - ly his
plea - sures, the po - lo, the hunt, And just like the rest he is
E♭° G7 D7 G7
dolce e più lento.
just now the thing, Or sees a new bon - net she likes oh! so
club must at tend? Who is it drinks bran - dy and smokes strong che -
off to the front; Al - tho' he's a John - ny, he'll fight in the
dolce e più lento.
C D7 G D11 D7
much, Her sim - ple re - mark is, "Now who can I touch?"
roots? Who is it that gets in - to bed in his boots?
ruck, He's weal - thy and fool - ish, but if you want pluck:
G C♯° G7 D7 G7
CHORUS. 1st time mf 2nd time ff.
What price Bur - ling - ton Ber - tie the boy with the Hyde Park
What price Bur - ling - ton Ber - tie the boy with the Hyde Park
What price Bur - ling - ton Ber - tie the boy with the Hyde Park
C G7 A7

drawl, . . . What price Bur - ling - ton Ber - tie the
drawl, . . . What price Bur - ling - ton Ber - tie the
drawl, . . . What price Bur - ling - ton Ber - tie the
G7
boy with the Bond Street crawl ? . . . A nice lit - tle sup - per at the Sa -
boy with the Bond Street crawl ? . . . He drives from his club : what a love - ly
boy with the Bond Street crawl ? . . . He'll fight and he'll die like an Eng - lish -
B7 Em G7 C G7 C G7
voy, oh ! what a duck of a boy, . . . " So free," says she, " with
sight ! the cabby says, " ere's a wet night," . . . " But free," says he, " with
man : forgive all his fol - ly we can, . . . Says old John Bull, " I
C D7 G G7 Am E7 Am A7
1st 2nd.
L. . . S. D. Bur - ling-ton Ber - tie's the boy for me." me."
L. . . S. D. Bur - ling-ton Ber - tie's the jay for me." me."
plain - ly see Bur - ling-ton boys are the boys for me ! " me."
G7 A Dm C G7 C Dm G7 C
D.C 𝄋

Girly-Girly

WRITTEN BY RICHARD MORTON AND G. M. COHAN. COMPOSED BY G. M. COHAN.

- on his gir - ly - gir - - ly. Though you try ..... to change to
love or in - di - ges - - tion. But the girl..... says "Yes," and
once vas cur - ly - cur - - ly. Then the ba - by comes, and
C7 F F7 B♭ F7
sub - ject yet, "He says you go a - long—"............ And he sings this
says it quick, And' he's a hap - py man; .... At the start he
that's a treat, It real - ly is a dear! .... But oh! if the
B♭ G7 Cm
cho - rus tacked on to His gir - ly, gir - ly song:—............
can't be - lieve his luck— But in a month he can! ....
bed is small and there's A ba - by ev - 'ry year! ....
A7 B♭ Gm C7 F7

CHORUS. 1st time p, 2nd time f.
My dear lit - tle girl - y - girl - y, Your hair is so nice and
For it's up in the morn - ing ear - ly, She lies in the bed so
No won - der the chap gets sur - ly, His head it goes whirl - y -
Bb F7 Bb F7
cur - - ly,.............. And ev - 'ry morn - ing ear - - ly I
sur - ly,— He's light - ing the fire for gir - ly, Who
- whir - ly, And ev - 'ry new boy and gir - ly, Takes
Bb C7
go my girl to see;........................ My heart it goes whir - ly
wants a cup of tea!........................ And he groans as he scrubs the
up some inch - es more;...................... Talk a - bout an - gry
F F7 Bb F7

- whir - - ly, Ev - ry - thing's hur - ly - bur - - ly,— With -
"air - - ey," "Oh, bach - e - lors all, be wa - - ry!" And be
ra - - ther,— Well you would get in a la - - ther, When be -
Bb G7 Cm
- out you gir - ly, gir - ly, What would this wide world
does a swea - ry, swea - ry, With such a big, big
- cause of the kids the fa - ther— Has to sleep on a nail in the
Eb6 E♮ o Bb Eb Bb C7 F7
1st time.
2nd time.
be? My be?....................
D.! For D.!....................
door! No door!..................
f
Bb Bb Bb F7
Bb Eb Bb C7 F7 Bb
Fine.
D.C.

Bill Bailey, Won't You Please Come Home

Words and Music by
HUGHIE CANNON

2
Won't you come home Bill Bail - ey won't you come home
Gm7 C7 F C7
She moans the whole day long Ba - by
F F#o C7 Gm7
I'll do the cook- ing dar- ling I'll pay the rent I know I've
C7 Gm7 C7 C7 Dm7 D#o C7 C7
(E bass)
done you wrong Come on hon - ey 'mem - ber that
C7+ F Dm7 Gm7 C7 F

rain - y eve - ning I drove you out with noth - ing but a
F C7 F
fine tooth comb (a fine tooth comb) I know I'm to
F7 Bb
blame well ain't that a shame? Bill Bail - ey won't you
Bbm F F7 (Eb bass) D7 Gm7
D.S.
FINE
please come home home.
C9 F6 C7 F6

Oh, I Must Go Home To-Night!

Written and Composed by WILLIAM HARGREAVES.

ad lib.
p
Jones was a fel - low who
Off to the station he
Out of the station he
Bb
went the pace with all his youthful might, And took a great de - light in
made a dash, to ask a-bout his train, To take him home a - gain— but
made a dive, and in the street did land, He yell'd and waved his hand, for a
Bb+ Bb F7
stay - ing out all night. When peo - ple were thinking of go - ing to bed a -
he asked all in vain. They said there's none running at all to-night to
tax - i off the stand. He gave his address to the dri - - ver and in
Bb F7 Bb Bb+
- round the West he'd roam, He'd go to Clubs or go to Pubs, but
where you want to go, All traf - fic is sus - pend - ed for the
con - fi-dence a - greed To give him half a sov' - reign if he
Bb F F+ F6 F+ F F+ F6 F+

ne - ver would go home...... But one night in - side the club he
line's block'd up with snow...... He walk'd up and down the plat - form
put on ex - tra speed...... But smash went the tax - i, for the
C7 F F7
gave his pals a fright,...... When he said "I'm go - ing home," and wish'd them all good -
a - ny - thing but gay,...... Said he "I would tramp home if I on - ly knew the
speed was far too high,...... Said Jones, "I don't live up here," as he shot in the
B♭ F 7 B♭
- night...... They thought that he was jok - ing and they all laugh'd out a -
way."...... A por - ter said, "You'll have to wait till morning I'm a -
sky...... He fell down on the pavement, and a p'liceman said be -
F7 F C7 F F°
- loud...... But Jones look'd ve - ry Se - rious as he shouted to the crowd:......
- fraid," But Jones said "That's im - pos - si - ble I can - not be de - layed."......
- lo, "We'll take you to the hos - pi - tal," but Jone - sy whispered "No:......
F Gm C7 F7

CHORUS.

"Oh, I must go home to - night,..... I must go home to - night,......... I
p - f
F7
B♭
don't care if it's snow - ing,- blow - ing,- I'm go - ing, I on - ly got married this
F7
B♭11 B♭
B♭ B♮°
morn - ing, it fills me with de - light,............... I'll stay out so long as you
C7
F F7
B♭
B♭ B♮°
like next week, But I must go home to - night!" "Oh, I night!"
1.
2.
f
ff
C7
F7
B♭
B♭
D.C. 𝄋

Give Me A Ticket To Heaven

Written by
RICHARD ELTON.

Composed by
DENHAM HARRISON.

In - to a rail - way - sta - tion crept a lit - tle child one night; The
p
E♭ B♭7 E♭ E♭° B♭
last train was just leav - ing, and the bus - tle at its height. The
E♭ Gm D7 Gm
sta - tion-mas - ter, stand - ing there, look'd down with won - d'ring eyes Up -
B♭7 E♭ B♭ E♭

- on this lit - tle maid,-so frail in form, so small in size. "Where
Cm F7 Eb C7 F7 Bb7 Eb
is your fa - ther, lit - tle one? Are you a - lone?" he cried. With
Cm C° Gm Cm C° Gm
Key Bb
tear - ful eyes she look'd up in his face, and thus re - plied,—
rit.
Ebm6 C7(b5) Bb C11 F 7 Bb7

CHORUS. 1st time p 2nd ff
Tempo di Valse.
"Give me a ticket to Hea - ven; That's where Dad's gone, they say................
He'll be so lone - ly with - out me, Tra - vel - ling all that way..............
Mother died when I was born, sir, And left Dad and me all a - lone;............ So
give me a ticket to Hea - ven, please, Be - fore the last train is gone."..........
Eb
Bb7
F7
Bb
Ab
Eb
Ab
G
Bb7
Eb
Fm
Bb11
Bb7
Eb
Andante moderato.
mf
Fine.
Eb
Ab7
Eb
B7
Eb
Cm7
Fm7
Bb7
Eb
D.C.

Pansy Faces

Words by
HARRY B. SMITH.

Music by
WILLIAM H. PENN.

Daintily.
1. There's a gar - den where the ro - ses red are bloom - ing,........... And per -
2. There the li - ly of the val - ley seems a - ring - ing,........... Bells a -
p
A♭
- fum - ing............... All the air.............................. It be -
- swing - ing,............. All for you.............................. There the
E♭7
- longs, with all its ar - bours cool and sha - dy,............... To my
mar - i - gold says, "Do not mar - ry gold, dear............ I am
B♭m7
E♭7
la - dy............... young and fair.................................... When she
told, dear,........... 'tis not true."................................ All a -
B♭m7
E♭7
A♭6

vis - its there as queen of all the ro - ses,............ And re -
- dore her, from the dai - sy al - most hid - den,............ That un -
Ab
- pos - es.................. for a while,............................ 'Tis the
- bid - den................ dares to love; .... But the
F7
Bbm
pret - ty pur - ple pan - sies that my la - dy loves the best, With their
pret - ty pur - ple pan - sies with their hu - man fa - ces turn, To
Bbm
Ab
fa - ces look - ing up to smile.................................
smile at her, their queen a - bove.................................
poco - - rit.
Bb7
Eb Eb° Eb7

CHORUS. 1st time p 2nd f
All the lit_tle pan_sy fa_ces,................. Grow_ing in the gar_den
there,.............................. Look for you with eyes of
long_ing,.............................. For you are their la_dy
fair;..................... And when you come out to greet them,............
Ped. ✻ Eb
Ab
Eb7
Ab
Ab
Ab
A♮
Eb7
Ped. ✻
Eb

Lean - ing like a queen a - bove,
Ab
poco rit.
All the lit - tle pan - sy fa - ces Look at you with eyes of
poco rit.
E°
Ab F7
Bbm
Eb11
Eb7
1.
D.S.
2.
love.
love.
mp
Ab
Ab
Ab
p
rit.
Bbm7 Eb 7
Ab D.C.

In The Good Old Summer Time

Words by
REN SHIELDS

Music by
GEORGE EVANS

trou-ble an-noy-ing, each one is en-joy-ing The good old sum-mer time.
go steal-ing cher-ries with face brown as ber-ries The good old sum-mer time.
E♭ E♮° B♭ C7 Gm7 G7 F C7 F Gm7 F
CHORUS
In the good old sum-mer time, In the good old sum-mer time,
B♭ B♭+ E♭ B♭ B♮° F7
Stroll-ing thro' the sha-dy lanes With your ba-by mine; You
B♭ D7 Gm Gm7 C7 F7
hold her hand and she holds yours, And thats a ve-ry good sign That
B♭ F Gm B♭ F7 C♯° B♭7 E♭ B♭
she's your toot-sy woot-sy In the good old sum-mer time
D.S.
B♭ F Gm7 Dm7 B♭ C7 E♭m6 F7 B♭

Sweet Adeline

Words by
RICHARD H. GERARD.

Music by
HARRY ARMSTRONG.

time love when you were near; It is then I won-der where you are, my
van - ished a dream gone by; If we meet sometime in af - ter years, my
mf
C7 Bb Bb Bb7 Eb Ebm
dar - ling, And if your heart to me is still the
dar - ling, I trust that I will find your love, still
Bb Gm C7
same, For the sigh - ing wind and night - in - gale a -
mine, Tho' my heart is sad, and clouds a - bove are
p
F7 Bb Eb Ebm6
- sing - ing Are breath - ing on - ly your own sweet name.
hov' - ring The sun, a - gain, love for me would shine.
Bb G7 C7 F7 Bb Eb Bb+ Bb

CHORUS.

Sweet A-del-ine, My A-del-ine At night, Dear
mf espressivo.
F7 Bb D7 Eb
heart For you I pine, In all my
F7 Bb F7
dreams, Your fair face beams, You're the
Bb D7 Eb Eo Eb
flow-er of my heart, Sweet A-del-ine.
Bb G7 C7 F7 Bb
D.C.

My Hero

English words by
STANISLAUS STANGE.

Music by
OSCAR STRAUS.

His like on earth who shall........ dis - cov - - - er?
It is my du - - - ty to love thee ev - - - er,
C G7 C C F#° E7 Am
rit.
a tempo
His heart is mine, and mine a - lone. We pledged our troth each
To love thee ev - er, love thee ev - er. We pledged our troth each
rit.
a tempo
C D7 G Am
to........... the oth - - - er, And for our hap - - pi -
to........... the oth - - - er, And for our hap - - pi -
D C G G Am

cresc.
ness........ I pray, Our lives........ be - long to
ness........ I pray, Our lives........ be - long to
cresc.
D7 C G C G7 C
rit.
one....... an - oth - er, Oh hap - py hap - py wed - ding day,
one....... an - oth - er, Oh hap - py hap - py wed - ding day,
C F♯° G7 C Am Cmaj7 F D11 G7 C
Oh hap - py, hap - - py wed - - ding day.
Oh hap - py, hap - - py wed - - ding day.
Am D7♭5 C G13 G7 C

Valse lento.
Come! Come! I love you on - - ly, My
sostenuto
C
D11
heart is true,.................. Come! Come! my life is
p cresc.
G7
C
G7
appassionato
lone - ly, I long for you.................. Come!
mf cresc.
C
Am
f
pp
Come! Naught can ef - face you, My arms are ach - ing
C
Dm7
G+

cresc.
now to em - brace you, Thou art di - vine!
cresc. allargando
C F Em Am Dm G7
f Broadly.
Come! Come! I love you on - ly Come, he - ro
f Broadly.
ff
C F Am Dm Am Dm Fm6
1.
mine
dim.
mf
p
p
C Cmaj7 Am D7 G7 G7
2.
mine
f a tempo
f
C (C) Am F Am C6 C

Wait Till The Sun Shines, Nellie

Words by
ANDREW B. STERLING

Music by
HARRY VON TILZER

REFRAIN
Marcia

Stop Yer Tickling, Jock!

Words by
HARRY LAUDER &
FRANK FOLLOY

Music by
HARRY LAUDER

cheeks they are a ro - sy red, And her age is just sweet
did en - joy my - sel' that day, And— I can tell ye,
faith - er and her mi - ther went To the kirk, which was a'
-cause I think she's just the sort Of—— lass to keep me
G
D
sev - en - teen. When I throw my arms a-
so did she! On the rail - way train, as
richt for me. What a love - ly, love - ly
nice and warm. I—— think she has a
ff
p
G
C
-round her neck And try to steal a kiss, Oh, she'll wriggle and gig-gle and
we went thro' The tun - nels in the dark, Oh, — ev - 'ry time I
feed we had Of ham and eggs and bun! Oh, and af - ter that we
lot o' brass, But that I'll find out soon, If she has, then we'll go
G
A7
D
D7
G
twist and twig-gle, And then you'll hear her— shout - ing this -
wink'd at her— The pas - sen - gers heard— her re - mark -
had some trea - cle Ro - ly po - ly—— just for fun.
ri - ding on— The 'Tup - p'ny Tube' for the hon - ey - moon.
D7
G

CHORUS
2nd time f
'Will yer stop yer tick-ling, Jock! Oh, stop yer tick-ling, Jock!
p
fz
G
D7
Di - na mak' me laugh so hear-ty, or you'll mak' me choke. Oh! I wish you'd stop yer
G
A7
D
D7
G
non-sense— just look at all the folk. Will yer stop yer tic-kle-ing
A7
D7
G
tic-kle-ic-kle-ic-kle-ing Stop yer tick-ling, Jock! " 'Will yer Jock!"
1
2
Fine
D
G
D
D7
G
D.C.

Nellie Dean

HARRY ARMSTRONG.

to the wa-ters flow, Nel - lie Dean. I can hear the rob-ins sing-ing Nel - lie
sol-dier boy you'd wed, Nel - lie Dean. All the world seems sad and lone-ly Nel - lie
F Bb F C7 F
Bb Eb F7 Bb Eb Gb°
Dean; Sweet-est re - col - lec - tions bring - ing Nel - lie
Dean; For I love you and you on - ly Nel - lie
Bb Gm Eb C#°
Dean. And they seem to sing of you With your
Dean. And I won - der if on high You still
D F7 Eb Ebm Bb
ten-der eyes of blue, For I know they miss you too, Nel - lie Dean.
love me if you sigh For the hap - py days gone by, Nel - lie Dean.
Eb Ebm Bb C7 F

CHORUS.

There's an old mill by the stream, Nel - lie Dean, Where we
p
Bb Bb7 Eb Ebm Bb
used to sit and dream, Nel - lie Dean. And the
Bb Bb° Cm7 F7
wa - ters as they flow Seem to mu - mur sweet and low, You're my
Bb Eb Bb C F7 D G7
hearts de - sire, I love you, Nel - lie Dean
C7 Bb F7sus4 F Bb Bb Bb
D.C. 𝄋

She's A Lassie From Lancashire

Written and Composed by C. W. MURPHY, DAN LIPTON and JOHN NEAT.

toil in U. S. A. When A-
mp
C7 F F7 Bb
mer - i - can girls gath - er'd round And sought his com - pa -
Eb Ebm6
- ny, He'd say "There's on -
Bb D7 Gm
- ly one girl for me"
rall.
C7 F

CHORUS.

She's a las-sie from Lan - ca - shire, Just a las-sie from
Lan - ca - shire, She's the las-sie that I love dear, Oh!
so dear.
Though she dres-ses in clogs and shawl,
She's the pret-ti - est of them all,
None could be fair-er or rar-er than
Sa-rah, My lass from Lan - ca - shire.
shire.
mp ff
mp
sf
D.S.
1
2
Bb
F
Bb F7 Bb
C7
F
Bb
F7
Bb F7 Bb
Bb Bb+ Eb F7 Bb Bb+
Eb F7 Bb C7
F7
Bb
F7 Eb F
Bb

Put On Your Old Grey Bonnet

Words by
STANLEY MURPHY

Music by
PERCY WENRICH

"Dear - ie don't be wea - ry, you were al - ways bright and cheer - y, But a
drove her up to Dov - er thro' the same old fields of clov - er, To be -
F
G7
tear, dear, dims your eye."______ Said she "they're tears of
come his hap - py bride.______ The birds were sweet - ly
C7
F B♭ F Cm7 F
G7
glad - ness, Si - las, they're not tears of sad - ness, It is fif - ty years to -
sing - ing And the same old bells were ring - ing, As they pass'd the quaint old
C
G7
C
D
day since we were wed."______ Then the old man's dim eyes bright - en'd, And his
church where they were wed.______ And that night when stars were gleam - ing, The old
G7
C F C7 D7 C7
F

stern old heart it light - en'd, As he turn'd to her and said,
cou - ple lay a dream - ing, Dream - ing of the words he said,
G7
C7
F Bb F Cm7 F
CHORUS.
"Put on your old grey bon-net with the blue rib - bon on it, While I hitch old
p-f
Bb
Eb
Bb
Dob-bin to the shay, And through the fields of clo-ver, We'll drive up to
C7
F7 Cm7 F7 Cm7 F7 Eb6 Bb F7 Bb D7 Gm7 Eb
1
2
Do-ver on our gold - en Wed - ding day." "Put on your
D.S.
f
Bb Gm Eb6 Bb C7 F7 Bb

Red Wing

(An Indian Fable)

Words by
THURLAND CHATTAWAY.

Music by
KERRY MILLS.

sang a lay, a love song gay, As on the plain she'd
un - der the sky, each night she would lie, And dream a - bout his
Bb7
Eb
Cm
F7
while a - way the day; She loved a war - rior bold, this
com - ing by and by; But when all the braves re - turned, the
Bb7
Eb
shy lit - tle maid of old, But brave and gay, he
heart of Red Wing yearned, For far, far a - way, her
Ab
Eb
Bb7
rode one day to bat - tle far a - way.
war - ri - or gay fell brave - ly in the fray.
Eb
F7
Bb7
Eb

CHORUS.

Now, the moon shines to - night on pret - ty Red Wing
mp - f
Ab
Eb
the breeze is sigh - ing, the night-birds cry - ing,
Bb7
Eb
For a - far 'neath his star her brave is sleep - ing,
Ab
Eb
While Red Wing's weep - ing her heart a -
Bb7
1.
way. Now, the
Eb
2.
way.
f
Eb

I Used To Sigh For The Silvery Moon

Words by
LESTER BARRETT

Music by
HERMANN E. DARBWSKI, Jun.

CHORUS

I used to sigh for the sil-v'ry moon, I used to
mp-f
Bass Tacet
A7
D
sigh for ma coal-black coon, I used to
A7
D
F♯7
spoon in the bright moon-light, And when the
B7
E7
moon was out of sight, I used to
A7
B♭o
A7
D

sing to ma Man-dy Lou, "Ma heart is sad
A7 D A7
but ma love is true." I've chang'd that tune,
D F♯7 B7
we were wed in June, We've a new moon now.
8va
E7 D
1 2
it's a hon-ey-moon. I used to -moon.
f
A7 D D
D.S.

Any Old Iron?

Written & Composed by
CHAS. COLLINS, E. A. SHEPPARD &
FRED TERRY

I put it on right a-cross my vest, Thought I look'd a dan - dy as it
Just then the Mayor he be-gan to smile, Saw my face and then he shou-ted
One of them said "We want a pot of ale Run him to the rag-shop, and we'll
I wore my chain on my dar-by kell, The sun was shin-ing on it and it
C F C C F C C
dan - gled on my chest. Just to flash it off I star - ted
"Lum - my what a dial!" Start - ed a Lord Mayor-ing and I
bung him on the scale. I heard the fel - low say "What's in this
made me look a swell. The or - gan start - ed play - ing and the
D7 G
wal - king round a - bout, A lot of kid-dies foll-ow'd me and all be-gan to shout:
thought that I should die When point-ing to my watch and chain he holl-er'd to me 'Hi!
bun - dle that you've got" Then whis-per to me kind-ly: "Do you want to lose your lot?
bells be - gan to ring, My chain be-gan to rat-tle, so the choir be-gan to sing.
B° D7 G

Chorus. (1st. time p 2nd. ff)
"An-y old iron an-y old iron An-y an-y old, old i-ron? You look neat
talk about a treat, You look dap-per from your nap-per to your feet. Dress'd in style,
brand new tile, And your fath-er's old green tie on, But I would-n't give you tup-pence for your
old watch chain, Old i-ron old i-ron? i-ron?
C F C C F C C F D7
G7 D7 G C F C
C F C C D7 G7 Am
C G7 C G7 C
1
2
D. C.

Let Me Call You Sweetheart

Words by
BETH SLATER WHITSON

Music by
LEO FRIEDMAN

When the sil - v'ry moon - light gleams, Still I
Birds are sing - ing far and near, Ro - ses
D Gm B♭+ B♭ C7
wan - der on in dreams, In a land of
bloom - ing ev - 'ry - where, You a - lone my
F7 B♭6 B♭m6
rall.
love, it seems, Just with you
heart can cheer, You, just you
rall.
F D7 G7 C7 F7
CHORUS
Let me call you "Sweet-heart," I'm in love with
p-f
B♭ B♭○ B♭ E♭ G7

you, Let me hear you whis-per that you love
C7 F7 A B♭
me too; Keep the love - light glow-ing In your
B○ F7 B♭ B♭○ B♭
eyes so true, Let me call you "Sweet-heart"
E♭ G7 C E♭ B♭○ B♭
1 2
I'm in love with you. you.
D. C.
E♭ E♭○ B♭ C7 F7 B♭ F7 B♭

Has Anybody Seen My Tiddler?

Written and Composed by

A. J. MILLS and
FRANK W. CARTER

caught a lit - tle tid - dler with a nice soft roe.
Dick - y push'd me in the pond, my socks got wet.
tried to kick the bot - tom out of my jam - jar.
F
Oh, how it wrig - gled in the jam - jar, There were
I said, "I'm goin' to tell your fa - ther, And we'll
He said he'd fol - low me to my street, And he
Gm
C7
F
C
F7
tears in its eyes of blue; ......
soon be on e - qual terms". ....
stuck to me just like glue. ......
Now I'm un - hap - py 'cos I've
He call'd me names to get his
All of a sud - den tho' I
B♭
A
C
G7
lost it, So ex - cuse me ask - ing you.
own back, And he col - lared all my worms.
miss'd him And I miss'd my tid - dler too.
C
Dm
G7
C7
Gm7
C7

CHORUS

Has any-body seen my tid-dle-er? tid-dle, id-dle, id-dle, id-dle,
mp–f
F C7 F Gm Cm Gm Cm
id-dle-er? I caught that little fish with some cotton and a pin; Oh! how I laugh'd when I
Gm D7 Gm D7 Gm D7 Gm
dragg'd him in, But com-ing home, oh dear, oh! That rude boy Dick-y Did-dle-er, He
Gm G7(5♭) C7 F C° C7 F B♭ F
1 2
poked his fingers in my gal-li-pot, and pinch'd my tid-dle-er. Has tid-dle-er.
mf sfz
F7 B♭ B♭m6 C C7 F C7 F
D.S.

When I Take My Morning Promenade

Written by
A.J. MILLS

Composed by
BENNETT SCOTT

change of leaf. She'd stare.... if she could come to town, Oh!
not much more. Fan - cy........ my dress - ing like that, too, The
must wear less. Each year..... our cos - tume grows more brief, I
D7 G G7 C
what would Mo - ther Eve think of my new Par - is - ian gown?
"Dai - ly Mir - ror" man would sure - ly want an in - ter - view.
won - der when we'll get back to the good old - fash - ioned leaf?
rall.
A7 Cm G D7 G
CHORUS
When I take my morn - ing prom - en - ade, Quite a fash - ion card, on the
p-f
C G7
Prom - en - ade. Oh! I don't mind nice boys star - ing hard, If it
C

sat - is - fies their de - sire. Do you think my dress is a
B7 G7 C
lit - tle bit, Just a lit - tle bit– Well– not too much of it, Tho' it
G7 C A7
shows my shape just a lit - tle bit, That's the
Dm A7 Dm G7 C G7 C C°
lit - tle bit the boys ad - mire. When I - mire.
D7 Fm6 G7 C G7 C
D.C.

I'm Twenty-One To-Day

Written and Composed by ALEC KENDAL.

fin - ished up with col - lege life; Now, I'm one of the boys. I
saw Queen Ma - ry, and the Shah, And sweet Red Rid - ing - Hood. I
he took me to Bow Street, where The judge said: "What's the case? What
play'd a game of bil - liards, To the mark - er, then, said I: "How
love to mar - ry you, young man, But, one thing's stop - ping me." She
C G Am A7 D11 D7
mean to paint the town, to - night, And give each girl a wink;
al - so saw the fat girl, there, And she cried, in a - larm: "I'd
has this great big bul - ly done?" His face grew quite a length. I
is the game? Please, tell me, sir!" He said: "You're twen - ty - three!" I
said: "Why don't you grow a beard?" I said: "May I be hung, I
G B7 Am A D D#° Em
Bri - tons nev - er shall be slaves; So, let your glass - es chink!
love to kiss your ba - by face!" I said: "Well, there's no harm!
said: "I smack'd the p'lice-man's face, I've o - ver - grown my strength!
said: "I don't wish to be rude, But, if you'll par - don me,
would - n't mind a fair moustache, But, for whis - kers, I'm too young!
F° L F D° A7 A° A7 D11 D7

CHORUS.

I'm twen - ty-one to-day! Twen - ty - one to-day!
p—mf
G B7 Am A D7 G
I've got the key of the door, Nev-er been twen - ty - one be-fore. And
G B♭° D7 D G° G D7
pa says I can do as I like; So shout, "Hip, hip, hoor-ay!
G B♭° D7 G Cmaj7 C Am
1. 2.
He's a jol-ly good fel - low, twen-ty-one to-day!" I'm twen-ty-one to-day!"
G C G D7 D11 D7 G D7 D11 D7 G

Alexander's Ragtime Band

Words and Music
By IRVING BERLIN

Oh, ma hon - ey, Let me take you to Al - ex - an - der's
Come and lis - ten, To a class - i - cal band what's peach - es,
C C7 F G7
grand stand, brass band, Ain't you com - in' a - long?
come now, some - how, Bet - ter hur - ry a - long.
C C7 F F#° C G7 C C7
CHORUS
Come on and hear, Come on and hear Al - ex - an - der's rag-time
p-f
F Dm7 C7
band, Come on and hear, Come on and hear, It's the best band in the
F Bb Gm7 B♭

band, ... They can play a bu - gle call like you nev - er heard be-fore,
F
So nat - ur - al that you want to go to war; That's just the
Fm6 C Eb°
best - est band what am, hon - ey lamb, Come on a -
G7 C C7 C7+
long, ... Come on a - long, ... Let me take you by the
F Dm7 C7

hand,........ Up to the man,......... Up to the man........... who's the lead - er of the
F Bb Gm7 Bb
band,............... And if you care to hear the Swa - nee Riv - er played in
F7 Cm F7 Cm7 F Bb
rag - time,...... Come on and hear,.............. Come on and hear.................. Al - ex -
G#° F Ab°
an - der's rag - time band............... Come on and, band...............
1 2 DS
C9 F F

There's A Long, Long Trail

Written by
STODDARD KING.

Composed by
ZO ELLIOTT.

list'_ning for your song. Old re_mem_brances are throng_ing
ev'_ry where I go. Tho' the road be_tween us stretch_es
Cm Bb7 Cm G7 Cm C7 Fm C7 Fm Db Fm
C7 Fm
Thro' my mem_o_ry. Throng_ing till it seems the
Man_y a wea_ry mile, Some-how I for_get that
pp
Fm C7 Fm Bbm Fm Bbm Fm
CHORUS
world is full of dreams Just to call you back to me. There's a
you're not with me yet When I think I see you smile.
Db Fm C7 Fm Bbm G7(b5) C
CHORUS
long, long trail a_wind_ing In_to the land of my dreams, Where the
f
pp
Ab C7 Fm Db Ab Eb7 Ab

night - in - gales are sing - ing And a white moon
pp
Db Ab Eb Ab Bb7
beams: There's a long, long night of wait - ing Un - til my
f
pp
Eb7 Bbm Eb7 Ab Db
dreams all come true; Till the day when I'll be
ff rit.
Ab Eb7 Ab Db
1
2
go - ing down That long, long trail with you. There's a you.
f
Ab Eb Ab Ab+ Ab Eb Ab Fo Eb7 Ab

Moonlight Bay

Words by
EDWARD MADDEN

Music by
PERCY WENRICH

CHORUS

We were sail-ing a - long On Moon-light Bay, We could hear the voi-ces
Bb Bb(7♮) Bb7 Bb+ Eb Ebm Bb
ring - ing, They seem to say "You have sto - len my heart,
F7 FO F7 Bb F7 Bb Bb(7♮)
Now don't go 'way!" As we sang Love's old sweet song, On Moon-light
Bb7 Bb+ Eb Ebm Bb Eb Bb F7
1
2
Bay. We were sail - ing a - Bay.
Bb Cm7 C#O Bb Bb Cm7 Bb6

Who Were You With Last Night?

Written and Composed by FRED GODFREY & MARK SHERIDAN.

Wan-dered in one Fri-day morn, In a brand new fan-cy vest. His pals all rose and
"You're mis-tak-en, boys, be-cause I was out with Un-cle Fred." His pals looked round and
They said "Wow-wow, O-ba-diah, you can tell that tale to Noah, We knew you by your
D7 B7 B7 Em Am7 D7
said "My word, you're a naugh-ty, naugh-ty boy. Last night we saw you mak-ing eyes at a
winked, then said, as they gave a know-ing grin, Do you al-ways squeeze your Un-cle's waist, and
spright-ly walk, and the tale you told was grand. Last night we saw you in the park there
Bm F♯m Bm F♯m F7 A7 B♭o
nice lit-tle lump of joy, You kissed her twice on the same place twice, and gave her waist a
tic-kle his brist-ly chin, Does your Un-cle, too, wear a high-heeled shoe, and a dain-ty powdered
list-'ning to the band. Your dar-ling wife, she would have your life, and put your hair in
E7 A C7 F A7
squeeze, So we'd like you to in-form us, Mis-ter O-ba-di-ah, please."
face, Does he sport a hob-ble skirt and bits of fur-be-lows and lace?"
curl, If she knew you'd been out walk-ing with some oth-er lit-tle girl!"
Dm F7 A D♯o A F♯7 Bm A Bm7 E7 A
sf

CHORUS *Not fast.*

The End Of My Old Cigar

Words and Music by
R.P. WESTON & WORTON DAVID

Allegro moderato.

smok'd it up till Eas - ter, then my dear de - vo - ted wife ______ Said,
then I saw an an - i - mal that caus'd a lot of chaff, ______ 'Twas
said, "If you send me out there, I'll stop their swank and bluff." ______ Then
C
C♯°
G
"Why not throw the end a - way?" I said, "Not on your life!" ______
called the "Um - ga - zoo - ze - lum," and just to make it laugh, ______
just to show my dig - ni - ty, I took an - oth - er puff ______
fz
Am
D7
G
Em
D7
CHORUS
With the end of my old ci - gar - Hoo - rah! hoo - rah! ______ hoo -
With the end of my old ci - gar - Hoo - rah! hoo - rah! ______ hoo -
With the end of my old ci - gar - Hoo - rah! hoo - rah! ______ hoo -
G
D7
rah! ______ I stroll up Pic - ca - dil - ly, and they fan - cy I'm the
rah! ______ I tick - led it be - neath the chin, and then the wife's mam -
rah!, ______ I said, "You leave this war to me, old cock and there you
G

Shah. I've kept it now for twenty - ty years to
ma Cried out, "It has - n't got a tail, it
are! If I can't kill 'em off with shells, they'll
G
do the "la di da," And I'd ra - ther lose my
does look sin - gu - lar!" So I bor - row'd a pin and
get a nas - ty jar. I'll poi - son the whole darn'd
D7
job than lose the end of my old ci - gar. With the
I stuck on the end of my old ci - gar. With the
lot of 'em with the end of my old ci - gar." At the
1
F°
D7
G
D7
2,3,4
D.S.
gar.
fz
ff
fz
fz
G
D7
G

4. I used to be a sailor, but when I was on the sea,
The vessel struck upon a rock just off the Zuyder Zee.
The captain yelled, "We're sinking!" but I said, "You're up the pole!"
And soon they saw your humble servant bunging up the hole.

Chorus

With the end of my old cigar - Hoorah! hoorah! hoorah!
I bunged the hole up in the ship and saved each jolly tar;
But soon they shouted "Fire!" but the cabin boy said "Bah!
He's under the boat and puffing away at the end of his old cigar."

5. To help the Prince of Wales' Fund, and do our little share,
We gave a swell bazaar down at the mission room, and there
My wife was selling kisses to the dukes and earls, it's true.
She charged them half a sov'reign each, and I was helping too

Chorus

With the end of my old cigar - Hoorah! hoorah! hoorah!
We got the Prince of Wales a thousand pounds at our bazaar.
The wife was selling kisses to the swells at "half a bar,"
And I was running a peepshow with the end of my old cigar.

6. As I was coming home one night I saw a house on fire.
I thought I'd show my courage that the ladies all admire;
So I climbed up a ladder, and the flames began to fight,
Then just to show how cool I was, I stopped to get a light

Chorus

For the end of my old cigar - Hoorah! hoorah! hoorah!
Then all at once my missis shouted, "Wake up, can't you, pa!
I told you not to smoke in bed, you fool, and there you are,
You've burnt a hole in your nightshirt with the end of your old cigar."

7. I went to good old Southend, and when night began to fall,
I thought I'd go and have a swim behind a cockle stall.
But there I found a lady who'd been washed up on the shore;
She'd nothing on but seaweed, so I took another draw.

Chorus

At the end of my old cigar - Hoorah! hoorah! hoorah!
She shouted out to me, "Oh, sir! I don't know who you are,
But give me something, do, to put around my fig - ah!"
So I gave her the "band" I'd taken off the end of my old cigar.

Let The Great Big World Keep Turning

Words by
CLIFFORD GREY.

Music by
NAT. D. AYER.

Some - one who was true as true could be, I'd
Come what may. I'm wait - ing for the call, It
Cm Bb7 Eb Cm
nev - er want to sigh. What would I give to -
holds no fears for me. May - be the day is
F7 Bb Eb D7
- day— Just to hear some-one soft - ly say?
near— When the thought of my heart I'll hear.
Gm Ebm Bb Cm7(b5) F13 Bb7
REFRAIN.
Let the great big world keep turning, Nev - er mind if I've got
p-f
Bb11 Bb7 Eb Ebmaj Eb6 Fm7 Bb7 Eb Bb Cm F7

you; For I on - ly know That I want you so, And there's
Bb7 Eb Eb+ Ab Eb Bbm6 C7
no one else will do. You have sim - ply set me
mp
F13 F3(aug9) F13 F7 Bb7 Bb11 Bb7 Eb Ebmaj 7 Eb6
yearn-ing, And for ev - er I'll be true. Let the great big world keep on
Fm7 Bb7 Eb Bb Cm F7 Bb7 Eb Eb+ Ab
1. 2.
turn - ing round, Now I've found some-one like you. Let the you.
rit.
Eb Cm B7 Eb F7 Bb7 Eb Bb11 Bb7 Eb
D.S.

When I Leave The World Behind

By IRVING BERLIN.

When he must pass a - way And leave his wealth be - hind.
Scenes of their childhood days, When they were sweet six - teen.
Eb Cm6 G D7 G D G Bb7
I have - n't an - y gold To leave when I grow old,
I'll leave them each a song To sing the whole day long,
Eb
Some-how it passed me by.
As toward the end they plod.
I'm ve - ry poor, but still
To ev - 'ry bro - ken heart
Bb6 C7 F7
I'll leave a pre-cious will When I must say good - bye.
With sor - row torn a - part, I'll leave the love of God.
Bb7

Chorus.
With feeling
I'll leave the sun - shine to the flow - ers, I'll leave the
p-f
Bb7
Bb6
spring - time to the trees; And to the
Eb
old folks I'll leave the mem - 'ries Of a
Eb
F#°
Fm7 Bb7
ba - by up - on their knees. I'll leave the
Eb

night time to the dream - ers, I'll leave the song birds to the
mp
Eb7 Ab F7
blind; I'll leave the moon a - bove To
Bb7 Eb G7+
those in love, When I leave the world be - hind, When
Fm6 Abm6 Eb Bb7 Eb Bbm6 C7
1. 2.
I leave the world be - hind. I'll leave the hind.
D.C.
Fm7 Bb7 Eb A° Bb7 E7

I Stopped, And I Looked, And I Listened

Words by
NAT. D. AYER and CLIFFORD GREY.

Music by
NAT. D. AYER.

mis - chiev - ous elf For I rath - er ex - pect a sur -
pal in the know, I thought it an ab - so - lute
set - tled for life For I've found my true soul - mate at
Fm6 F G G7
- prise. T'oth - er day I was walk - ing a - long - side a hedge, A
cert. The cry came 'They're off' and my frame fair - ly shook For my
last. The first year of bliss was a dream of de - light, Ye
C C7 F6
hedge by the side of some trees; I got my sur - prise as I
horse was lead - ing the way, When op - o - site me it gave
God's, but my joy was su - preme. Till af - ter cu - cum - ber for
C11 F6 F Fm6
walk'd by the edge; 'Twas a sound waft - ed right o'er the breeze. So I
me such a look, And it paused in a cu - ri - ous way. It
sup - per one night, She start - ed to talk in a dream. So I
C A7 D7 G C

REFRAIN.
stopp'd and I look'd and I lis-ten'd, And I
stopp'd and it look'd and it lis-ten'd, I could
stopp'd and I look'd and I lis-ten'd, For the
G C7 F
tried to lo-cate the sound. First I thought it was here Then I
see it was think-ing of me, 'Twas pen-sive and sad, And it
case was un-ique you'll al low. I was fill'd with a-maze, I was
C7 F F C+
thought it was there. A most pe - cu-li-ar sound, And I real-ly de-clare That I'd
thought "Now for-sooth, It's ap - par-ent to me, If I win it's the truth, It
knock'd of a heap For I had no i-dea That she talk'd in her sleep, But I
F Dm G C
heard it be-fore, But I can-not tell where, So I thought that this noise must be
may be the ru-in of this fool-ish youth, It may teach him to risk L. S.
knew it was best, Per-fect si-lence to keep, For I thought I must hear this some-
F C G7 C D7 G7

found. So I stopp'd and I look'd and I lis-ten'd;
D." So it stopp'd and it look'd and it lis-ten'd;
-how. So I stopp'd and I look'd and I lis-ten'd;
C G7 C7 F
The sound seem'd to come from the ground, Someone said 'You'-
A light in its eyes I could see, Then it thought
8
And the sweat seem'd to stand on my brow- "My own dar-ling Joe"- "I
F F7 F° B♭m F
some-one said, 'Won't' Some-one said 'Do'- some-one said 'Don't' So I
"It's a sin, Per-haps I ought - not to win" And it
love you," she said "I wor-ship you so"- Well, as my name is Fred I
C7 Dm F7 B♭ B♭m♮7 F
stopp'd and I look'd and I lis - ten'd.
stopp'd and it look'd and I lost.
stopp'd, and I look'd and I- (To Audience) Think it over!
fz
D.C.
G7 C7 F

Good-Bye-Ee!

Written and Composed by
R.P. WESTON & BERT LEE

gay As the train mov'd out he said, "Re - mem - ber
Lynne" As the lit - tle dy - ing child Up - on his
knew Then she made a speech and said, "I look up -
G D7 G G○ G
me to all the Birds!" Then he wagg'd his paw, and went a -
snow white bed he lay, And a - mid their tears the peo - ple
-on you boys with pride, And for what you've done I'm going to
D F○ A7
-way to war, Shout - ing out these pa - thet - ic words, "Good -
gave three cheers When he said as he pass'd a - way.
kiss each one!" Then they all grabb'd their sticks and cried.
D A7 D7 Am7 D7

CHORUS
-bye-ee! good-bye-ee! Wipe the tear baby dear, from your eye-ee Tho' it's
G Am D7 G
hard to part, I know, I'll be tickled to death to go. Don't cry-ee! don't
C D7 G D A A7 D7 G
sigh-ee! There's a silver lining in the sky-ee. Bonsoir, old thing! cheer-i-
Am D7 G D7 G E7
-o! chin-chin! Nah-poo! Too-dle-oo! Good-bye-ee!" "Good-bye-ee!"
Am E7 Am D7 G D7 G

For Me And My Gal

Words by
EDGAR LESLIE
& E. RAY GOETZ

Music by
GEO. W. MEYER

boy. In his wed-ding ar - ray Hear him smil-ing-ly say:
nite. Gee! it makes the boy proud As he says to the crowd:
C Em7 Am7 F9 E9 E9(♭9) A7 D7 D11 D7
CHORUS
"The bells are ring - ing for me and my gal, The birds are
p
mf
3
Am7 D7 G
sing - ing for me and my gal. Ev-'ry-bo-dy's been know - ing
Am D7 G B7 Em6
To a wedding they're go - ing And for weeks they've been sew - ing, Ev-'ry Susie and
B7 Em B7 Em Em7 A7 Dm A° A7

Sal. They're con-gra - gat - ing for me and my gal,
D7 D11 D7 Am7 D7 G
The Par-sons wait - ing for me and my gal, And some time
Am D7 B Em6 B° B7 D7 G°
I'm goin' to build a lit-tle home for two, For three or four or more, In
G7 Dm7 G7 C G° G♯°
Love - land for me and my gal." "The bells are gal."
1. 2.
D7 Am7 D7 G Em D7 G
D.C.

Smilin' Through

Words and Music by

ARTHUR A. PENN.

Slowly and simply.

ten.
lit - tle green gate At whose trel - lis I wait, While two
D F° A B7 E Gm6
rit.
eyes o' blue Come smil-in' through At me! There's a
rit.
mf accel.
mp a tempo.
D Em7 A7 D Em7 A7 D
gray lock or two in the brown of the hair. There's some
D D(#7) D7 G(#7) G6 G(#7) A7 A11 A7 D

sil - ver in mine, too, I see;............................ But in
cresc.
D D(♯7) D7 G(♯7) G6 E7 A
ten.
all the long years When the clouds brought their tears, Those two
rit.
p
D F° A7 B7 Em Em6
eyes o' blue Kept smil-in' through At me!............................
D. C.
D Em7 A D E7 A D

SMILIN' THROUGH

There's a little brown road windin' over the hill
To a little white cot by the sea;
There's a little green gate
At whose trellis I wait,
While two eyes o' blue
Come smilin' through
At me!

There's a gray lock or two in the brown of the hair,
There's some silver in mine, too, I see;
But in all the long years
When the clouds brought their tears,
Those two eyes o'blue
Kept smilin' through
At me!

And if ever I'm left in this world all alone,
I shall wait for my call patiently;
For if Heaven be kind,
I shall wake there to find
Those two eyes o'blue
Still smilin' through
At me!

Arthur A. Penn.

If You're Irish Come Into The Parlour

Written and Composed by SHAUN GLENVILLE and FRANK MILLER

Moderato

luck in for-eign parts he thought he'd try. Now he's made his
she got in - to trou - ble thro' her jaw. Six po - lice they
A7 D
name.... and is a wealth-y man,..... He put a bit a - way for a rain y
had...... to take her to the court,.... She was informed a month she would have to
G Em A7 C7
day; So if you gaze up - on......... The house of Pat-rick
do; So Pat-rick quick-ly wrote.... Up to the judge, a
B A7 D
John,........ You'll find a no - tice that goes on to say.
note,........ Ex - plain - ing, Sir, I'm much o - bliged to you!
A7 D D° A7 D D° D7

CHORUS

If you're I - rish........ come in - to the par - lour, There's a
wel - come there for you;............................ If your name
is Tim - o - thy or Pat,.......... So long as you come from
Ire - land. There's a wel - come on the mat. If you come from........
G A7 D7
G G° D7
G D Dm
A7 D D7 G

the moun-tains of Mourne, Or Kil - lar - ney's
A7 D7
lakes so blue, We'll sing you a song and we'll
D7+ G G○ G
make a fuss, Who - ev - er you are you are one of us, If you're I - rish,
D7 G D7 G D7 G D7 G
1 2
this is the place for you! If you're you!
f
Am7 D7 G D7 G
D.S.

I'm Forever

Blowing Bubbles

JAAN KENBROVIN &
JOHN WILLIAM KELLETTE.

CHORUS.

I'm ...... for-ev - er blow - ing bub-bles, ... Pret - ty bub-bles in the
p–f
B♭ B♭ E♭
air, ... They fly so high, near-ly reach the sky, Then like my
B♭ E♭ B♭ E♭ B♭ C7 F♯°
dreams they fade and die. For - tune's al - ways hid - ing, ...
C7 F7 B♭ B♭m B♭ D7 D11 D7
I've looked ev - 'ry - where, ... I'm .... for-ev - er blow - ing bub-bles, ...
Gm E♭7 D7 F7 F9 B♭ F7 B♭
..... Pret-ty bub-bles in the air. .... air. ....
1. 2.
D. C.
C7 F7 B♭ B♭

I Belong To Glasgow

Written and Composed by WILL FYFFE.

PATTER *(follows 1st time Chorus after 2nd Verse)*

I might not be able to *sing* that song, but the subject's good *(hic)*. The man that takes a drink, he's a man. When you're teetotal, you've got a rotten feeling that everybody's your boss. I am here to-night as the representative of the British working man. And I'm going to tell you, fellow workmen *(addressing an imaginary crowd,)* that in the future we have been too bloomin' slow, but in the past, we will show them what we mean to do. There must be no holding back *(staggers)*. Our motto now is "Steady, boys, steady." Why should these bloomin' millionaires have all the money? Give it to *me*. Do you know what I'm going to tell ye? Their money's tainted. *Tainted! 'Taint* yours, *'taint* mine. It belongs to them, and they're going to bloomin' well keep it. Yet they condemn a poor British working man, because they see him staggering down the road, drunk. Why? What's he going to do? The poor chap's got to *get home*. What about these people in their bloomin' motor-cars? They go past so quick, you don't know whether they're drunk or sober. It's all wrong. I ought to know, because —

Repeat Chorus.

Three O'clock In The Morning

Words by
DOROTHY TERRISS

Music by
JULIAN ROBLEDO

I could keep dancing with you for ev-er, dear, just with you.
There goes the three o' clock chime, Chim - - ing, rhym - - ing, My heart keeps beat-ing in time,
Sounds like a sweet lov-er's tune,
Tell me soon we will be on our hon - ey - moon, It's
Both hands 2 octaves higher
loco
mf Chimes
p
A7 Dm B7 C G7 C D7 G7 C
D7 G D7
Ddim D7 G
D7 B
E7 Am A7 D7 G

three o'-clock in the morn - ing, We've danced all the whole night through; And
day-light soon will be dawn - - ing, Just one more waltz with you............ That
mel - o - dy so en - tranc - ing, Seems to be made for us two,...........
I could keep danc - ing with you for ev - er, dear, just with you..........
C G7 C Cdim C G7 C Caug F A7 Dm B7 C G7 C D7 G7 C
Both hands 2 octaves higher
loco
mf Chimes
sf
sf

Let The Rest Of The World Go By

Words by
J. KEIRN BRENNAN

Music by
ERNEST R. BALL

REFRAIN *Tenderly with expression*

peace, Where joys nev-er cease, Out there be-neath a
E♭7
kind - ly sky
kind - ly sky, We'll build a sweet lit - tle
C Fm C A♭
nest some - where in the west, And let the rest of the
E♭7
porta
1
2
D.C.
world go by. With by.
A♭ B♮° E♭7 E♭maj 7 A♭
+5

Don't Have Any More Missus Moore

Written and Composed by HARRY CASTLING & JAMES WALSH.

CHORUS.

Don't have a - ny more, Missus Moore,........................ Mis-sus Moore, please don't have a - ny
p-f
Bb Ebm6 E♮o Bb Eb Bb Bb+
more.......................... The more you have the more you want, they say, But e - nough is as
Eb G7 Cm F7 Bb D7 Gm Bbm6 F
If you have ma - ny more, Mis-sus Moore,........................ You'll
good as a feast a - ny day. If you have ma - ny more, Mis-sus Moore,........................ You'll
If you have ma - ny more, Mis-sus Moore,........................ I
C7 F C7 G#o F Bb Ebm Bb Ebo Bb
have to rent the house next door.......................... They're al-right when they're here but take my ad-vice old
ne-ver get to your street door.......................... Too ma - ny double gins give the ladies double
don't know what we'll do, I'm sure.......................... Our churchyard is so small there'll be no room for them
Bb7 Bb+ Eb G7 Cm Ebm Bb D7 Eb Eo
dear, Don't have a - ny more, Mis - sus Moore. Moore..................
chins, So don't have a - ny more, Mis - sus Moore. Moore..................
all, So don't have a - ny more, Mis - sus Moore. Moore..................
1. 2.
f
Bb F7 Bb Bb7 C7 A7 Bb Bb+ Cm F7 Bb D.S.

Every Little Movement

by MOORE

That's why the La - dy is re - sid - ing in town.
F7
F7
B♭7
Twelve months a - go her mod - est self felt quite sub - lime to
E♭m
A♭m6
sit on a fel - low's knee who's been in all the grime! And if
A♭m6
you should want a kiss, She'd drop her eyes like this, But
D♭7
G♭
D♭7
G♭

now she drop them just one at a time.
Gm7 C7 F7 B♭7
And Ev - ery lit - tle move - ment has a mean - ing of it's
E♭ A♭6
own, Ev - ery lit - tle move - ment tells a tale.
B♭7 E♭ E♮o
When she walks in daint - y
B♭7 G7 A♭ Cm

hob - bles, at the back round here, theres a kind of wib - ble wob - ble
F7
Bb7
And she glides like this Then the
Eb
C7
John - nies fol - low in her trail 'cos when she
Fm
Bb
Bb7
(Spoken)
turns her head like so, Some - things go - ing don't you know,
Eb
Bb7
Eb
Bb
Eb

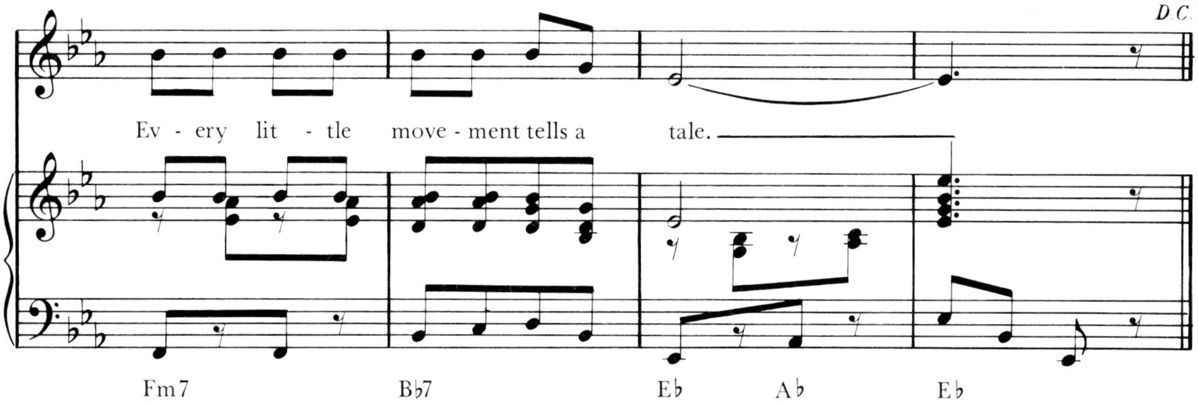

Chorus And every little movement has a meaning of its own,
Every little movement tells a tale.
When she walks in dainty hobbles,
At the back round here, there's a kind of wibble-wobble;
And she glides like this,
Then the Johnnies follow in her trail,
'Cos when she turns her head like so,
Something's going, don't you know,
Every little movement tells a tale.

2. Down by the blue sea, cute as she could be,
Maudie would go for her dip every day.
Maudie has an eye for the boys, Oh my!
And it happens that Reggie was passing that way.
When Reggie saw her he fell into a trance,
He too is going bathing for her now, here's a chance.
She didn't smile or frown,
Just threw her signal down!
Then slyly shrugged her shoulders with a glance.

Chorus And every little movement has a meaning of its own,
Every little movement tells a tale.
When she dashed into the ocean,
Reggie kept close by for to know her
Maudie tried to swim:
"Oh I'm here," said Reggie, "if you fail,"
And in less than half a wink,
Maudie dear commenced to sink,
Every little movement tells a tale.

3. Congratulations, such celebrations,
Bertie and Gertie have just tied the knot.
Both at the party, all gay and hearty,
And noticed the bridegroom looks anxious, eh what?
When friends and relatives depart their different ways,
Alone with the girlie of his heart.
And once again he turned the lights down low,
She looked at him like so,
Then shyly with her wedding ring she played.

Chorus And every little movement has a meaning of its own,
Every little movement tells a tale.
When alone no words they utter,
But when midnight chimed, then their hearts begin to flutter.
And she yawned like this,
And stretches out her arm so frail,
And her hubby full of love,
Looks at her and points above,
Every little movement tells a tale.

On Mother Kelly's Doorstep

Words and Music by
GEO. A. STEVENS

both sit down on a door-step there And we'd pic-ture the fu-ture grand.
wash-day, hold-ing her pail, was Ma-ry The milk-maid milk-ing cows.
F7 Bb F7 Bb
CHORUS
On Moth-er Kel-ly door-step, down Par-a-dise Row I'd sit a-long o' Nel-ly,
p-f
Fm7 Bb7 Eb Eb° Bb7
she'd sit a-long o' Joe. She'd got a lit-tle hole in her frock, hole in her shoe,
Eb Cm Gm
Hole in her sock, where her toe peep'd through, But Nel-ly was the smart-est down our
Ab Eb Gb7 Bb F7

Al - ley. On Moth-er Kel-ly's door - step, I'm won-der-ing now
B♭ Fm7 B♭ E♭
If li'l gal Nel - ly re-mem-bers Joe, her beau, And does she
F♯o B♭ E♭ A♭m E♭ Fm7 B♭7
love me like she used to, On Moth-er Kel-ly's door - step,
Cm D7 Ao E♭ Fm7 B♭7
1 2
D.C.
down Par-a-dise Row. On Moth-er Kel-ly's
f
E♭ A♭ B♭7 E♭ F♯o E♭

Riding On Top Of The Car

Words by
FRED LEIGH & V.B. BRYAN

Music by
HARRY VON TILZER

Tempo di Valse.

ve - ry best place for a "spoon;" An old rus - tic stile must be
G7 C C#o G7 C A7
there, they'll ex - plain, And not too much light from the moon. Now,
Dm F#o G7 C
my girl and I live in town, you must know, Where quiet coun - try lanes can't be
G D7 G C#o D7
found; We've no rus - tic stiles in our neigh - bour - hood,
G C G7 C A7 Dm

rall.
D.%.
so Ev - 'ry time Sun - day ev - 'ning comes round
rall.
F♯° G7 C G G11 G° G7
CHORUS.
Then we go go go for a ride on the
p f
C E7 Am G C
car car car, For we know how
F A7 Dm G7
co - sy the tops of the tram - cars are The
C C♯° G7

seats are so small, and there's not much to pay, You sit close to - geth - er and
C C+ Dm
"spoon" all the way. There's man - y a Miss will be Mis - sis some day Thro'
G7 C Am C
1 2
rid - ing on top of the car Then we car
f
D7 G7 C G7 C
D.%.
f
Fine.
C Am C D7 G7 C

2. We climb on the car where the journey begins
And we make for the first vacant seat.
For all other people we don't care two pins
So long as our comfort's complete.
And when the conductor comes up for the fares,
He punches our tickets, then goes,
But gives us a wink as he pops down the stairs,
Like an overgrown Cupid, in clothes

3. We get to the end of the journey all right,
Or, at least, to the end of the track.
But while all the others prepare to alight,
We remain on the car, and go back.
And when we get married now, boys, here's a tip
That ought to be useful to you
We shan't spent too much on our honeymoon-trip,
For we've made up our minds what to do

Are We To Part Like This, Bill?

Words and Music by
HARRY CASTLING
CHARLES COLLINS

None can guess how I felt at the sight, With tears in my eyes, that I
I ne - ver thought that he'd turn a - gainst me, When I'm sleep - ing or wak - ing, at
A7 A+ D B♭+ D G C7
tried to keep back, I crept to his side and said:
work or at home, I find my - self murmuring this:
rall.
D7 E7 A7 F♯m E9/A A7 D11 D7
CHORUS
Are we to part like this, Bill, Are we to part this way?
f-p
G C♯o G G E7 Am
Who's it to be, 'er or me? Don't be a - fraid to
Cm D7 D7+

3. Down in a little laundry
Me and 'er work side by side every day;
She was my pal, and I looked to 'er well,
Trusted and helped 'er in every way;
Still, if my Bill cares for 'er more than me,
I wish 'em no harm—no, but prosperetee;
I try to forget him, but each day I find
These words running through my mind.

What Did She Know About Railways?

Written by
C. G. COTES

Composed by
BENNETT SCOTT

Moderato
Allegro
jump'd up-on the en-gine but the stok-er push'd her down; But what did she know a-bout
make her un-der-stand the por-ters took no end of pains; But what did she know a-bout
p Moderato
mf Allegro
D7 G° G A7 G
Moderato
rail-ways? The guard came up and spoke to her, as she stood sob-bing there, Asked
rail-ways? When she got to the bar-ri-er, an ar-gu-ment a-rose, The
mf Moderato
D7 G D A7 D A7
her if she'd a tick-et, but she answer'd with a stare; Said he "You can't go up to town un-
man said "I must punch your ticket," spoke sharp, I suppose; Said she "Thou punch my ticket and I'll
D B7 Em7
Allegro
-til you've paid your fare." But what did she know a-bout rail-ways?
punch thee on thy nose." But what did she know a-bout rail-ways?
Allegro
A7 D A7 D

CHORUS

3

The porters all got on to her and asked her then and there,
"What do you know about railways?"
Then she pitched into all the lot and soon their faces were
Covered all over with railways.
Some police then came upon the scene and seized her "rolling stock",
Next morning twelve black-eyed porters stood by – she was in the dock,
And when the beak said, "fourteen days," it gave her such a shock,
She nearly fell through her railways.

CHORUS: She arrived at Euston &c.

I'm Just Wild About Harry

Lyrics by NOBLE SISSLE

Music by EUBIE BLAKE

Allegro moderato

Chorus:

I'm Just Wild A - bout Har - ry, And Har - ry's wild
C Dm7 G7 Dm7 G7 Dm7 G7
a - bout me, The heav'n - ly bliss - es
Dm7 G7 C G7 Cdim C
of his kiss - es Fill me with ec - sta - sy,
Dm7 Fm6 C G7+5 C Gdim
He's sweet, just like choc-'late can - dy, And
G7 G6 C Dm7 G7 Dm7

just like hon - ey from the bee,
Oh, I'm Just Wild
About Har - ry And he's just wild a - bout,
can - not do with - out He's just wild a - bout
me.
me.
(opt.)
b.c.
1
2
G7 Dm7 G7 Dm7 G7 Am Ab+ C Dm D7
Adim Em G+ Em7 A7 Cm6 G7 C F6 F G7
C Fm6 Fm Fm6 C Fm6 F G7
C Cdim C Cdim G7 C6 C Cdim G7 C

Down At The Old Bull And Bush

Words by
RUSSELL HUNTING, PERCY KRONE
and ANDREW B. STIRLING

Music by
HARRY VON TILZER

You know the place, it has won great re - nown. Of - ten with my
She would not change with the Queen and her crown. It was there I
D7 G D7 G7 C
sweet-heart on a bright sum-mer's day To the lit-tle pub there my
first met the joy of my life, She gave her troth and is
C7 F A7 Dm G7
foot-steps will stray, If she hes-it-ates when she looks at the
now my dear wife. Her eyes al-ways glis-ten when she sees the old
C C♯° G7 C G7
sign, Promptly I whis-per, "Now, do not de - cline."
sign, So all of you join in a glass of good wine.
D7 G7 D7 G D7 G7

Come, come, come and make eyes at me Down at the old Bull and Bush. Come,
C F C G7
come drink some port wine with me Down at the old Bull and Bush (Bush, Bush) Hear the lit-tle
C G7 C
Ger-man Band, Just let me hold your hand, dear. Do,
F C F C
do come and have a drink or two Down at the old Bull and Bush (Bush, Bush.) Bush (Bush, Bush.)
F G7 C C
1
2

The Songs

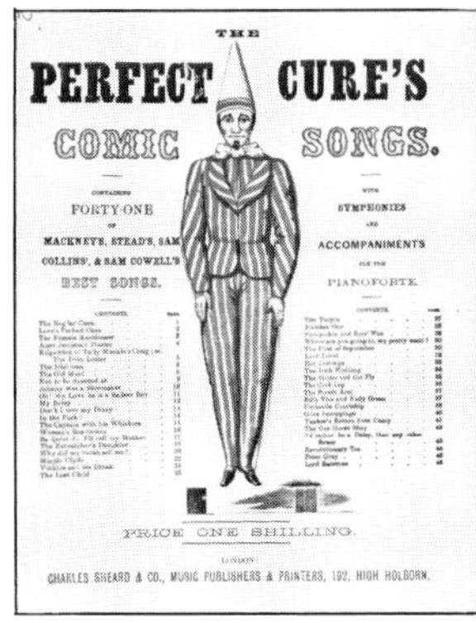

VILIKINS AND HIS DINAH. Music and words anonymous. First known publication was in London in 1853. Frederick Robson sang it in a musical farce, 'The Wandering Minstrel', in 1836, but it had a longer history as *William and Dinah*. Appeared in various British and American editions with various spellings, but was given wide popularity by the Irish comedian Sam Cowell (1820–64) who re-published it in his 'New Universal Illustrated Pocket Songster' (*c.* 1856), his 'The Comic Vocalist' (*c.* 1861) and '120 Comic Songs' (*c.* 1850). It was also printed in the 'Musical Bouquet' series by Charles Sheard. It had a further lease of life in America in a version by John A. Stone as *Sweet Betsy from Pike* first published in 1858. Recorded by Alfie Bass (World Records (S) ST797); John Foreman (Reality RY1004).

THE MERMAID. Music by Alfred Lee (dates unknown). Words by William Makepeace Thackeray (1811–63). The original of this song was 'known among a select circle to be an Impromptu of the late Mr. Thackeray' improvised one evening at one of the song-and-supper rooms. It made use of a traditional melody and a quote from Arne's *Rule Britannia*. The item was transcribed by one of Thackeray's friends and published as No. 4672/3 in Sheard's 'Musical Bouquet' series *c.* 1870 and included in a volume, 'The "Champion" Comic Singer's 21 New Comic Songs, Motto Songs, and Parodies'. It was taken up by Arthur Lloyd (1839–1904) and sung by him in many London halls. Alfred Lee was a very prolific American composer who settled in London and provided the music for many hit songs of the 1860s and thereafter. Recorded by Stanley Holloway (World Records (S) ST325); John Foreman (Reality RY1004).

CHAMPAGNE CHARLIE. Music by Alfred Lee. Words by George Leybourne. This was the song by means of which Leybourne promoted Moët's famous champagne for a retainer in kind. It became very much his 'masher' signature tune and an early example, if not the first, of the advertising commercial. At this time Leybourne was earning £30 a week at the Canterbury, but soon after the Oxford was paying him £120. It was partly the champagne that made his merry life a short one. Recorded by Stanley Holloway (World Records (S) ST325); Charles Young (World Records (S) ST797).

THE MAN ON THE FLYING TRAPEZE. Music by Alfred Lee. Words by George Leybourne (1842–84). The French aerial performer Léotard (1842–70) credited as the inventor of the 'flying trapeze' and immortalised by the practical brief garment that he wore, was the star of the Cirque Franconi in Paris. When he appeared at the London

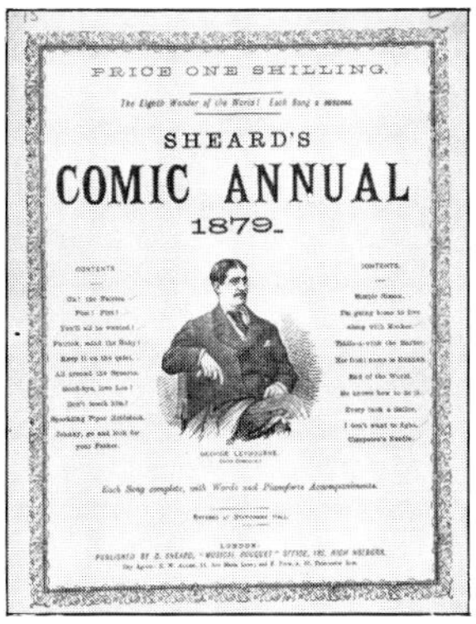

Alhambra in 1861 he became the talk of the town, and made successful return appearances in 1866 and 1868. In 1868, while he was earning £180 a week at the Alhambra, George Leybourne, dubbed by J. J. Poole 'the Lion Comique', collaborated with Alfred Lee on this song which cashed in on Léotard's popularity.

OH, THE FAIRIES. Music by W. G. Eaton. Words by T. S. Lonsdale. A popular skit on the ballet craze at the Alhambra in the 1870s, it was a favourite audience participation song at the Canterbury and elsewhere. Published as No. 5858/9 in the 'Musical Bouquet' series, it was included in Sheard's Comic Annual for 1879. In more recent years it has become the favourite participation chorus at the Players' Theatre. Recorded by Clive Dunn (Decca (S) SCL1238).

HE'S GOING TO MARRY MARY ANN. Music and words by Joseph Tabrar (1857–1931). Joseph Tabrar was a typical hack writer of the music-hall period. He began his musical career singing at Evans's and with the Moore & Burgess Minstrels for whom he wrote his first songs. He became a professional songwriter and turned out thousands of songs on demand. His biggest success was *Daddy wouldn't buy me a bow-wow**† which he wrote for Vesta Victoria. He also provided jokes, sketches, pantomimes, monologues and had a high opinion of his creative abilities. He had a large songwriting shop in the Waterloo Road and set many apprentice songsmiths on their way. The present song, a gay and unsentimental piece immortalising the legendary Mary Ann, was written for Bessie Bellwood (1857–96) and was included in Francis & Day's 4th Comic Album in 1885.

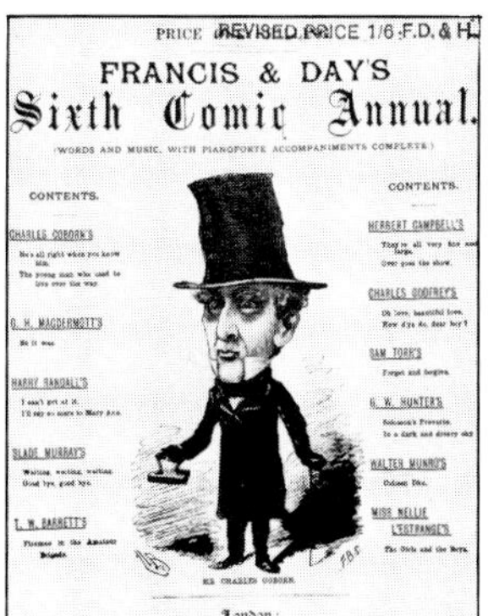

HE'S ALL RIGHT WHEN YOU KNOW HIM. Music and words by Charles Coborn. Charles Coborn (1852–1945) has perpetuated his image in the song *The Man Who Broke the bank at Monte Carlo**†, but he had a wide range of character studies to offer. Up to about 1880 he had mainly sung songs made famous by other people; after that he started to write his own, with a speciality in songs exploiting the French lingo. One of his best working-man songs was the one included here with its immortal line 'he's all right when you know him, but you've got to know him *fust*'. It was published in Francis & Day's 6th Comic Album in 1887. Coborn was an influential figure in the music-hall world, ever fighting for artiste's rights and helping to form the Music Hall Artiste's Association in 1885. Recorded by Charles Coborn (Music for Pleasure MFP1146).

YOUNG MEN TAKEN IN AND DONE FOR. Music and words by Harry King. The superb comedian and pantomime dame Dan Leno (1860–1904) had few of the more lasting music-hall songs in his repertoire, able to rely for his fame on his great acting and comical ability, his sketches and character studies. This is the one song to which his name is attached that is still well known. It was printed in Francis & Day's 9th Comic Annual in 1889.

THE TIN GEE-GEE or **THE LOWTHER ARCADE.** Music and words by Fred Cape (*c.* 1895). This song is interesting for its reference to the Lowther Arcade, a popular shopping precinct off the Strand in the late 19th century, and for its Victorian drawing-room type sentimentality. It was an immensely popular number in its time, leading a double life in the halls where it was sung by Fanny Wentworth and in the politer circles of the concert-hall where it was rendered with great success by Mel B. Spurr. These slightly 'higher-class' performers (like George Grossmith Sr, and Corney Grain) were usually greatly concerned to see that their repertoire was not lowered by use in the music halls.

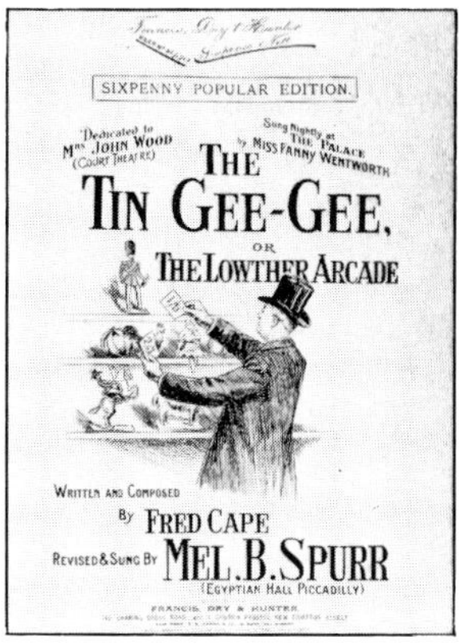

THE FUTURE MRS 'AWKINS. Music and words by Albert Chevalier (1861–1923). Chevalier was a skilful character actor who toured for most of the time with his own company, singing his famous Cockney songs and acting his Cockney sketches. If he was not, as he said, at heart a music-hall comedian, he still had a considerable success in the halls and earned the title of 'the Cockney Laureate'. He married the daughter of George Leybourne. He became best known for songs like *My old dutch** and *The future Mrs 'Awkins* put over in his 'quaint and pathetic manner' which won the approval of Mrs Ormiston Chant (the Mrs Whitehouse of the day) who found them a great improvement on the 'boozy and hateful songs' generally heard in the music halls. He wrote *Mrs 'Awkins* in digs in Brighton in 1892 in the company of the comedian G. W. Hunter. It has a splendid introduction and verse and was included in 'Albert Chevalier's Song Album, No. 1' (Reynolds, *c.* 1892). Recorded by Albert Chevalier (World Records SH350); Bill Owen (Decca (S) SCL1238); Robert Swann (Saga (S) SOC1042).

SWEET ROSIE O'GRADY. Music and words by Maude Nugent (1877–1958). Credited to the well-known singer and dancer at Johnny Reilly's 'The Abbey' on New York's Eighth Avenue, it is likely that it was partly the work of her husband William Jerome (1865–1932) who was a prolific songwriter and a music publisher. It is very much in his style and Maude Nugent never wrote anything else comparable. She signed away the rights to one publisher in 1896 and to another when the copyright was renewable in 1924 which resulted in some involved legal wrangles. She sued 20th Century Fox for using the song in the film of the same title starring Betty Grable after they had already paid one publisher for the rights. Recorded by Marie Kendall (Decca PA81).

SONS OF THE SEA. Music and words by Felix McGlennon (1856–1943). The writer was of Irish origin and, after an early writing career in England, went to America where he continued a prolific output of music hall and vaudeville songs, two of his greatest successes being *Her golden hair was hanging down her back** (1884) and *Comrades*† (1887). His *Sons of the sea* was sung with great patriotic fervour and to 'immense applause' by Arthur Reece, who built his reputation during the Boer War period with songs of a sentimentally

flag-waving nature like *Break the news to Mother*; *The Boers have got my Daddy*; *Bury her picture with me* and especially *The wedding bells shall not ring out tonight. Sons of the Sea* was written in 1897 and appeared in Sheard's 25th Comic Album. Arthur Reece was still singing it in 1935 at the Royal Command Variety Performance (World Records SH244).

OUR LODGER'S SUCH A NICE YOUNG MAN. Music and Words by Fred Murray and Laurence Barclay. A prime example of the saucy kind of song put over by the famous music-hall ladies like Marie Lloyd and Vesta Victoria (1874–1951) who made this particular song her own. She was the daughter of Joe Lawrence, proprietor of the Empire Music Hall in Cardiff, a small vivacious person who had an excellent ear for a good hit song – her other successes included *Daddy wouldn't buy me a bow-wow*†; *Waiting at the Church** and *Poor John**. She performed *Our lodger* with sweet innocence, the prototype of many such helpless young ladies who have such an appeal for helpful young men. The song was included in Francis & Day's '17th Comic Album' in 1898.

I'LL BE YOUR SWEETHEART. Music and words by Harry Dacre (1860–1922). Written in 1899 by the composer of *Daisy Bell**† (1892), one of the best known of all music-hall songs. Dacre went to America and became a prolific and successful songwriter with hundreds of titles to his credit and founded the Frank Dean Publishing Company. *I'll be your sweetheart* quickly became a favourite chorus number that filtered back to the British music hall. Recorded by Marie Kendall (Decca PA81); Beryl Reid (Music for Pleasure (S) MFP50174).

HELLO! MA BABY. Music by Joe Howard (1878–1961). Words by Ida Emerson. By 1899 the first ragtime craze was well on its way, built on the pioneer work of the classic black composers like Scott Joplin, and Tin Pan Alley was not slow to cash in with songs based on the captivating new rhythms. One of the earliest hits in this vein was *Hello! ma baby* which is also notable for an early reference to the telephone as a means of romantic communication – quite apart from a catchy and almost quintessential vaudeville type tune. Joe Howard himself became an American musical comedy star and a favourite of the Diamond Horseshoe and was always the best interpreter of this classic which he wrote with his wife. He had a great hit in 1905 with *I wonder who's kissing her now*. Recorded by the Frank Barber Shop Quartet (Music for Pleasure (S) MFP1375).

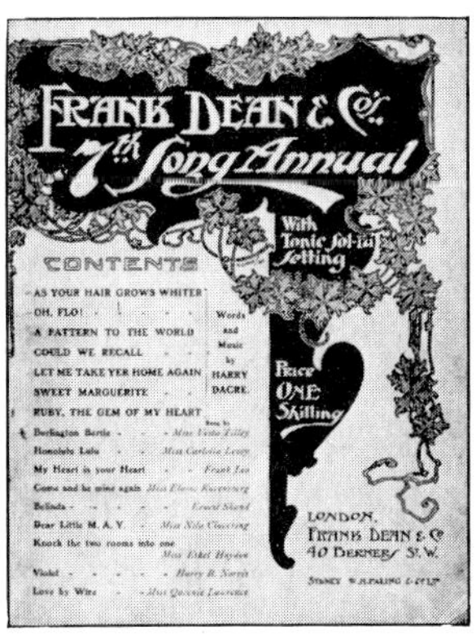

BURLINGTON BERTIE. Music and words by Harry B. Norris. The greatest of all the male impersonators, in spite of strong claims for other talented ladies, was almost certainly Vesta Tilley (1864–1952). Paradoxically, she had such feminine charm that it came through her saucy young men roles and she ended up by delighting both sexes. Ever since Lord George Cavendish had built the Burlington Arcade, as a sort of no-man's-land between Burlington House and the hoipolloi of Piccadilly, the name had taken on a sort of airs and graces association. Vesta Tilley's 'masher' song *Burlington Bertie* (1900) is not to be confused with the excellent take-off that Ella Shield's husband William Hargreaves wrote for her – *Burlington Bertie from Bow*: it has a less effective tune but the characterisation of Bertie 'the boy with the Hyde Park drawl' is excellent.

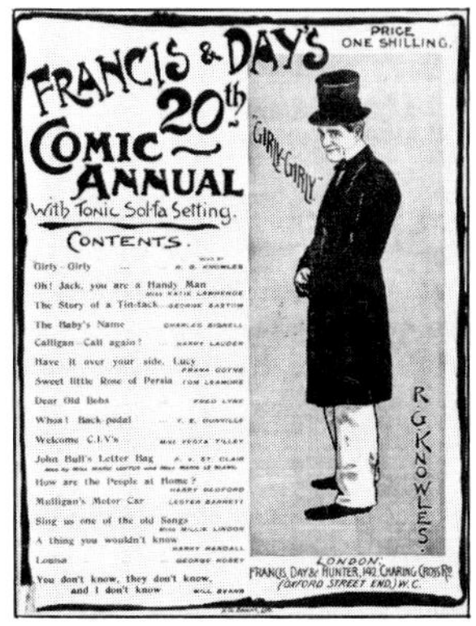

GIRLY-GIRLY. Music by [G. M.] Cohan. Words by Richard Morton and [G. M.] Cohan. Actually, written in 1899 by 'Jerry' Cohan of the American vaudeville act 'Jerry Cohan and his Six Irish Coleens' – the father of the famous George M. Cohan – it was the most successful hit in the musical repertoire of the 'very peculiar American comedian' R. G. Knowles (1858–1919) – who was born in Canada. He developed a style of humour that was a sustained sarcastic attack on the audience and he was one of the first to introduce the now familiar Bob-Hope-style wisecracking American routine to British audiences. He first appeared in London at the Trocadero in 1891, was at first greeted in stony silence but by the end of the act he had caught on. He made his home in England and was a top star of the halls for some twenty-five years.

BILL BAILEY, WON'T YOU PLEASE COME HOME. Music and Words by Hughie Cannon (1877–1912). Written in 1902, this is in the current ragtime idiom that swept the world. It has a tragicomic story behind it. The original Bill Bailey, a music teacher married to Sarah (who celebrated her 100th birthday in 1973), was a convivial man who liked to linger at the Whistler Bar in Jackson, Michigan, and received the traditional welcome from his wife when he arrived home late. He confided this to the pianist of the establishment, Hughie Cannon, who was immediately inspired to write the immortal song with its model by his side. It became a nation-wide hit and made Mrs Bailey's domestic situation so unbearable that she divorced Bill in 1910 and married a local farmer two years later. Bill Bailey died in 1954. Hughie Cannon sold his song outright for £170 and had no other comparable successes. Recorded by Burt Sheppard (1903) (Saydisc SDL-112).

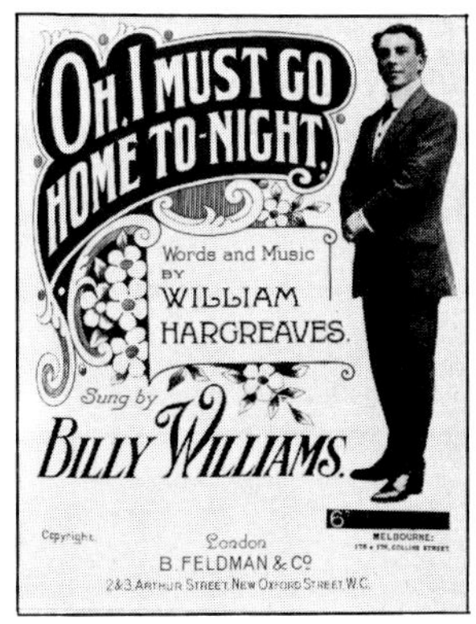

OH, I MUST GO HOME TONIGHT! Music and words by William Hargreaves. Hargreaves, husband of Ella Shield, was one of those prolific and reliable composers who turned out, with little public acclaim, a type of song that set the music-hall style around the turn of the century. The present song, in *Bill Bailey* vein, has a typical British 6/8 jauntiness and the classic lines: 'I only got married this morning; it fills me with delight . . . I'll stay out as long as you like next week, but I must go home tonight'. It was in the repertoire of the Australian comic Billy Williams (1878–1915) who came to England in 1900 and became known as 'The Man in the Velvet Suit', his usual smart attire. He was an early recording star, one of his songs *When Father papered the parlour** appearing on some thirty different labels.

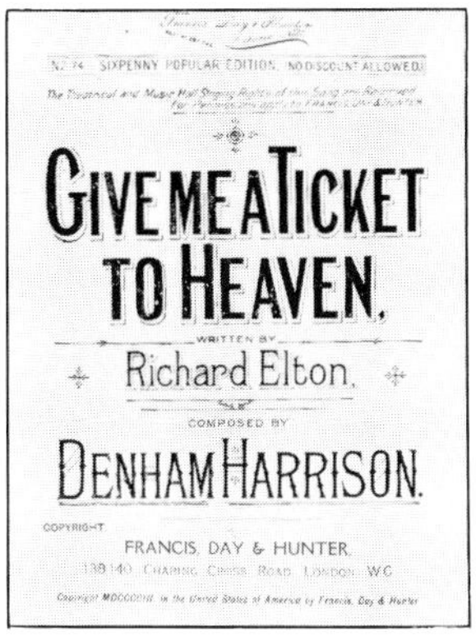

GIVE ME A TICKET TO HEAVEN. Music by Denham Harrison. Words by Richard Elton. Although dated 1902 this song has something of the 1870/80 character about it, with its sob story, so often heard with tearful enjoyment, of the orphan child. It is difficult for it not to descend into bathos, as with the last line, 'give me a ticket to Heaven, please, before the last train is gone' (railway travel was, of course, much cheaper then), and such songs required great art. The music-hall audience was notably sympathetic to such appeals to the heart and were wont to help the performer along with accompanying groans and sighs. Recorded by Benjamin Luxon (Argo (S) ZFB95/6).

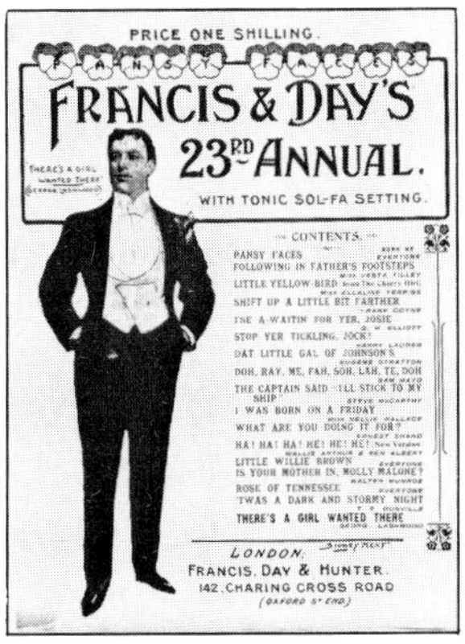

PANSY FACES. Music by William H. Penn. Words by Harry B. Smith (1860–1936). The name of William H. Penn is chiefly immortalised by that delightful song *The honeysuckle and the bee*† which Ellaline Terriss made famous in Britain. Harry Bache Smith was one of a family of American writers who started out as a newspaper journalist, found a flair for writing for the stage and finished up writing some 300 shows with such collaborators as Reginald De Koven, Victor Herbert, Jerome Kern, Ludwig Englander and Irving Berlin. Recorded by Benjamin Luxon (EMI (S) EMD 5528).

IN THE GOOD OLD SUMMER TIME. Music by George Evans (1870–1915). Words by Ren Shields (1868–1913). George 'Honey Boy' Evans, born in Wales, went to America when he was 7 and was one of the great stars of the American blackface minstrel shows. The song was said to have been written one day in 1902 when Evans and Shields were having a picnic at Brighton Beach (near Coney Island) with the popular music hall entertainer Blanche Ring. A remark by Evans that 'there was nothing like the good old summer time' immediately suggested a song which was completed a few days later in New York's Union Square Hotel. It was made famous by Blanche Ring, became a popular barber-shop number, and soon filtered over to the British Isles. Recorded by the Frank Barber Shop Quartet (Music for Pleasure (S) MFP1375); Julie Mackay (World Records SH350).

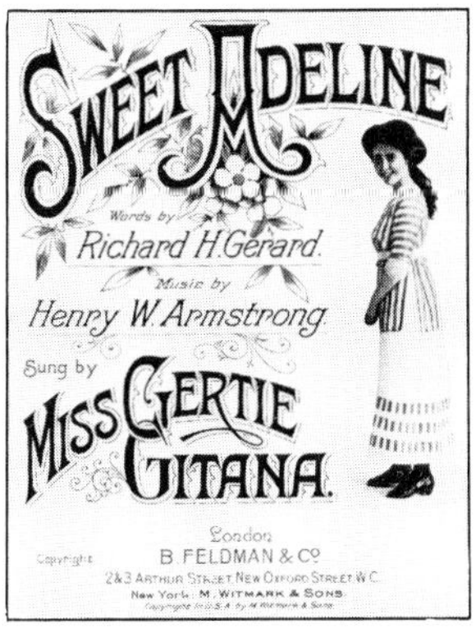

SWEET ADELINE. Music by Henry W. Armstrong (1879–1951). Words by Richard H. Gerard (1876–1948). The barber-shop quartet tradition is essentially an American tradition but similar close harmony groups (generally singing waiters) were an early attraction in the British music hall at the Oxford and elsewhere. *Sweet Adeline* is a classic of the genre. Harry Armstrong originally wrote the melody in 1896, calling it *Down home in old New England*, and Gerard's lyric was originally *Sweet Rosalie*. Inspired by the opera singer Adelina Patti, the importantly right title was found and the song as we know it was first published in 1903 and sung by Harry Ernest and the Quaker City Quartette. It became such a success that Armstrong, hitherto a booking agent and producer, was able to launch himself on a career as a vaudeville entertainer with it. Recorded by the Four Singing Waiters (World Records (S) ST667).

MY HERO. Music by Oscar Straus (1870–1954). Words by Stanislaus Stange. It is not completely stepping outside the field of variety entertainment to include one or two ballads and songs drawn from the wider musical theatre. A time-honoured part of musical-hall entertainment (as we have noted previously in the book) was the interpolation of some more 'serious' items to supply a bit of cultural uplift. Such a song as *My hero* (which often crops up in the 'Good Old Days' revivals) would have drawn respectful attention when sung by any talented soprano on the bill. It comes from 'The Chocolate Soldier', Straus's adaptation of Bernard Shaw's 'Arms and the Man', done without the playwright's blessing, first produced in 1908. Recorded by Robert Shaw Chorale (RCA DPS2059).

WAIT TILL THE SUN SHINES, NELLIE. Music by Harry Von Tilzer (1872–1946). Words by Andrew B. Sterling (1874–1955). Harry Von Tilzer (sometimes confused with his equally successful brother Albert) was one of the top American writers for vaudeville around the turn of the century. By 1905, when he wrote *Wait till the sun shines, Nellie*, the ragtime flavour was strong in his songs; the verse has an almost pure ragtime style – the chorus moves forward into a jazzier vein. It was a happy inspiration, the composer's own favourite and one of his most lucrative publications (he was also a publisher). It was motivated by a newspaper story about a poverty-stricken East Side family whom the writer cheered by promises of sunshine after the storm. Recorded by the Frank Barber Shop Quartet (Music for Pleasure (S) MFP1375); Joan Morris (Nonesuch (S) H-71304); Bing Crosby; and many others.

STOP YER TICKLING, JOCK! Music by Harry Lauder (1870–1950). Words by Harry Lauder and Frank Folloy. Starting out in life as a coal-miner, Harry Lauder became an amateur entertainer, writing his own songs, and launched out on a music-hall career in the North of England. At £7 a week he made his London début at Gatti's Music Hall and, in spite of the Scottish accent, was an immediate success. At the height of his career he was to earn £1000 a week. He was an excellent singer and provided himself with a range of fine songs like *I love a lassie*,*† *Roamin' in the gloamin'** and *Keep right on to the end of the road*. Here we have one in his sauciest vein which he wrote in 1904, recalling that richly human entertainer in full fling. Recorded by Harry Lauder (World Records SHB22; World Records SH199).

NELLIE DEAN. Music and words by Henry W. Armstrong (1879–1951). Already noted as the composer of *Sweet Adeline*, Harry Armstrong proved himself the dean of barber-shop writers by penning another supreme classic in this field, *Nellie Dean*, in 1906. It became even more popular in England in the 1900s than it did in America and was regularly promoted in the British music hall by the 'dainty comedienne' Gertie Gitana (1888–1957) who won the hearts of all who saw her and became a fashionable rage. She sang it with a sweeter

touch than it tends to get nowadays and its title became her billing – 'sweet Nellie Dean'. She had a great success at the Lyceum when that theatre was briefly a music hall. Recorded by the Four Singing Waiters (World Records (S) ST667); Gertie Gitana (World Records SH350).

SHE'S A LASSIE FROM LANCASHIRE. Music and words by C. W. Murphy (1875–1913), Dan Lipton and John Neat. Written in 1907, it was one of the songs taken up and popularised by that great lady of the music hall, Florrie Forde (1876–1940), who, like so many stars of the concert hall and music hall alike, came from Australia. Like her closest rival and exact contemporary Vesta Victoria, she had a great sense of choosing the rightest and best songs – *Oh, oh, Antonio*; *Hold your hand out, naughty boy; Down at the old Bull and Bush** were amongst her best and she lightened the war years with *Pack up your troubles*; *Take me back to dear old Blighty* and *Tipperary**. Recorded by Florrie Forde (Decca PA81) (Music for Pleasure MFP1146).

PUT ON YOUR OLD GREY BONNET. Music by Percy Wenrich (1880–1952). Words by Stanley Murphy (1875–1919). Wenrich published his first composition at his own expense when he was 17 before working in the music-publishing business and making his mark, first of all, with various ragtime compositions. His three big song hits were *Put on your old grey bonnet* (1909); *Moonlight Bay* (1912) and *When you wore a tulip* (1914). It has easily slipped into the community song class and is as well known in England as it is in America; any song with a final line about 'our golden wedding day' can be relied on to move the common spirit, and 'thro' fields of clover, we'll drive up to Dover' is neatly adaptable.

RED WING. Music by Kerry Mills (1869–1948). Words by Thurland Chattaway (1872–1947). This neat and merry little song, with its lyric about 'the little Indian maid' very quickly became a hit in America and came over the Atlantic not only as a song but in great use as an instrumental piece. The more than obvious hint of Schumann's *Merry peasant* probably helped it on its way. It had a later life in War years as *The sun shines bright on Charlie Chaplin.* Kerry Mills was already well known as a composer of classic cakewalk tunes like *At a Georgia camp-meeting* and *Whistling Rufus* and he was also a successful music-publisher. Recorded by Murray Johnson (World Records SH130).

I USED TO SIGH FOR THE SILVERY MOON. Music by Herman Darewski (1883–1947). Words by Lester Barrett. Darewski was a popular writer of marches and songs, contributing such classics as *In the twi-twi-twilight*† to the music hall. In 1904 he joined Francis, Day & Hunter but left to form his own publishing business in 1916. He prospered by buying up the Sheard catalogue but, finding things difficult after the War, sold out to Bert Feldman. Darewski had a long career as an orchestral and theatre conductor. He wrote the present song in 1909 and it was popularised by G. H. Elliott (1884–1962), the 'Chocolate Coloured Coon' who carried on the blackface tradition of

Eugene Stratton (1861–1914), and became his most famous number in the 'soft-shoe-shuffle' style. He also revived many of Leslie Stuart's songs.

ANY OLD IRON. Music and words by Charles Collins, E. A. Sheppard and Fred Terry. 1910. A special team were required to turn out the rapid patter songs which were the exuberant speciality of that prototype music-hall star Harry Champion (1866–1942). His ability to pack more words into the minute than anyone else and his sheer zest come over well even in the later recordings that he made – the old spirit of the halls came to life with him in the 1935 Royal Command Variety Performance. He was the last of the true 'red-nosed' comics and was especially popular with the patrons of the Old Middlesex Hall, familiarly known as the Old Mo. Recorded by Harry Champion (World Records SH244).

LET ME CALL YOU SWEETHEART. Music by Leo Friedman (1869–1927). Words by Beth Slater Whitson (1879–1930). Friedman was another songwriter/publisher who founded his fortune on one best-selling number, *Meet me in Dreamland* (1909) (with the same collaborator), but he was fortunate in following it up with something even better. *Let me call you sweetheart* immortalises a common phrase in the right musical terms and is likely to survive wherever people gather in sentimental and singing mood. These two songs between them sold something like ten million copies by the 1940s.

HAS ANYBODY SEEN MY TIDDLER Music and words by A. J. Mills (d. 1919) and Frank W. Carter. Part of the true vulgar tradition of music-hall song was the suggestive humour, never more successful then when it was put over with an air of innocence. Such songs as *With my little wigger-wagger in my hand* and *Whenever I touched my seaweed* were classics of the genre and the tradition continued into the thirties with George Formby's *Little stick of Blackpool rock*. It was never done with a lighter or more innocent air than in this little known but delightful song in which Millie Payne told the audience of that naughty boy who 'poked his fingers in my gallipot, and pinch'd my tiddler'.

WHEN I TAKE MY MORNING PROMENADE. Music by Bennett Scott (1875–1930). Words by A. J. Mills. 1910. An unusually graceful, well-turned melody for two unsung writers of various minor music-hall songs. It could well grace a sophisticated product of the operetta stage. As it was it became a saucy vehicle for the naughty talents of one of the music hall's greatest stars, Marie Lloyd (1870–1922), 'the Queen of the halls'. It is easy to imagine what sly zest she used when she confessed that her dress was 'a little bit' on the brief side revealing 'the little bit the boys admire'. Played with the right gentle lilt, it is a delightful song. For other Marie Lloyd items see a volume devoted to her numbers in The Music Makers series (EMI Publishing, 1977). Recorded by Marie

Lloyd (Rhapsody RHA6014); Patricia Rowlands (Decca (S) SCL1238).

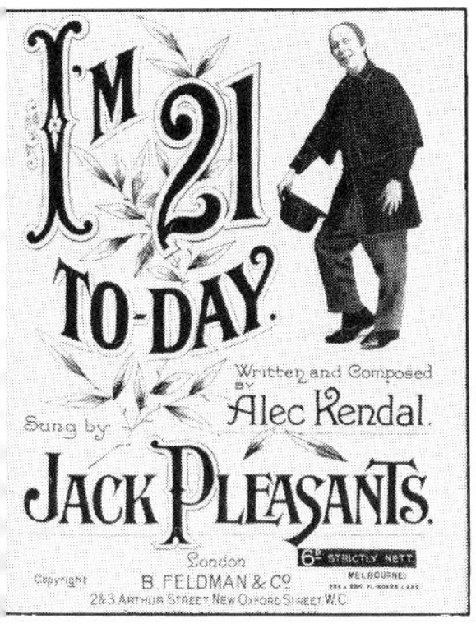

I'M TWENTY-ONE TODAY. Music and words by Alec Kendal. Convivial songs like *Happy birthday to you* and *For he's a jolly good fellow* tend to have a mixture of the hearty and the coy about them. *I'm twenty-one today* tends to be better not only because it is sung twenty-one times less than most anniversary songs but because it has a certain flippant and humorous quality about it. This is because it set out in life as a genuine music-hall song intended as a humorous comment on life rather than a song for an occasion and it was made famous by that master of being the shy, embarrassed young man, Jack Pleasants (1875–1924), who also sang *I'm shy, Mary Ellen.** Recorded by Jack Pleasants (World Records SHB43).

ALEXANDER'S RAGTIME BAND. Music and words by Irving Berlin (b. 1888). By 1911 there was already a second generation of ragtime songs to spark off a new revival – this time a positive craze. The world went foxtrot, cakewalk, twostep mad and one of the men most responsible was the Russian emigrant American composer Irving Berlin with songs like *Everybody's doin' it* and especially *Alexander's Ragtime Band.* Tin Pan Alley found a way of containing the ragtime characteristics in a popular form with those 'it's a bear, it's a bear, it's a bear' interpolations. The composer himself had first introduced the song at the Annual Friars Club show in 1911 without causing much stir and Eddie Miller and Helen Vincent both sang it in public before it was made a hit by Emma Carus. Recorded by Gottlieb's Orchestra (World Records SH275); Julie Andrews (CBS 62405); Burl Ives (WRC ST515).

THERE'S A LONG, LONG TRAIL. Music by Zo Elliott (1891–1964). Words by Stoddard King (1889–1933). (1913). There is a tendency to confuse this with Novello's *Keep the home fires burning* – it has a similar approach, sentiment and rhythm. Also taken up as a community-sung 'war' song. Its origins were vaguely academic. The words by Stoddard King won a Yale University literary prize and a competition was organised, the prize a tour with the Yale Glee Club, for the student who could write the best tune for it. One Alonzo Elliott won, but found no American publisher interested in the result. Elliott came to England to study at Oxford and found a publisher, West & Co. in London. The outbreak of war found the tune ideal in sentiment for an Army marching song and it became thought of as a 'war-time' song and immensely popular.

MOONLIGHT BAY. Music by Percy Wenrich (1880–1952). Words by Edward Madden (1878–1952). Published in 1912, it was one of Wenrich's biggest hits (another was *When you wore a tulip*), yet another of those American vaudeville songs that seem conceived and predestined for the barber-shop treatment (such songs must always have space between the phrases for an echoing phrase). Wenrich made his early reputation as ragtime composer and pianist and much of his early output was in that vein. Later, after the success of some of his songs like *Moonlight Bay* he wrote for the New York stage and had a notable hit with a show called 'Castles in the Air' in 1926. Recorded by the Frank Barber Shop Quartet (Music for Pleasure (S) MFP1375).

WHO WERE YOU WITH LAST NIGHT. (1912) Music and words by Fred Godfrey and Mark Sheridan (1867–1918). This is one of the finest 'rattling good choruses' in the music-hall repertoire. Its melody is absolutely right for the personal attacking approach on the audience who are being asked the question, including that powerfully upsurging 'ah, ah, ah . . .' in the middle. It should be noted by interpreters that the last night is grammatically 'who you were with last night'. It goes at a rattling pace with its raggy characteristics emphasised by the linking riffs in the piano accompaniment. Mark Sheridan, who had a fine powerful voice and enjoyed having a go at the audience, was one of the early grotesque comedians who dressed in an eccentric style as part of their act. Recorded by Beryl Reid (Music for Pleasure (S) MFP50174).

THE END OF MY OLD CIGAR. Music and words by R. P. Weston and Worton David. This was written in 1914 (with one hint of war clouds in it) to satisfy the insatiable need of Harry Champion (1866–1942) for rapid patter songs dealing with his main preoccupation – the good things in life like food, drink and a smoke. One can almost see these two sterling Tin Pan Alley hacks trying to put the necessary pace and sparkle into their immortal lines and melody, which they did very successfully. It was later categorised by one writer as an 'idiotic' song but this was never a drawback in the world of entertainment. Like many of the period it gives a lively portrait of social life of the times in its verses – the 'ninepenny' cigar, strolling up Piccadilly, the Zoo, Lord Kitchener, the Germans, the Prince of Wales' Fund, etc. Recorded by Harry Champion (Music for Pleasure MFP1146).

LET THE GREAT BIG WORLD KEEP TURNING. Music by Nat D. Ayer (1887–1952). Words by Clifford Grey (1887–1941). 'The Bing Boys Are Here' was such a success (with 378 performances which was a great deal for those days; 'Chu Chin Chow' was to hold the record for several decades with 2238) that it had to continue, being a revue, in what amounted to a new edition. So the sequel was 'The Bing Girls Are There'. Robey and Lester were not available (Robey came back with 'The Bing Boys on Broadway' in 1918) so were replaced by Wilkie Bard, Joseph Coyne and Laddie Cliff, but Violet Loraine was still the lead and needed another *If you were the only girl in the world**. The writers duly obliged with the only slightly less popular *Let the great big world keep turning* which Loraine turned into another wartime hit.

WHEN I LEAVE THIS WORLD BEHIND. Music and words by Irving Berlin (b. 1888). By 1915, when this song was penned, Irving Berlin had really got into his stride as possibly the world's most prolific songwriter, a title that would not have much significance if he was not

also one of the very best. These were days long before the 'classic' period of the 1920s and 1930s and the eventual writing of fine stage works like 'Annie Get Your Gun' and 'Call Me Madam'. Berlin turned his hand to all kinds of hits, specialising in the fashion of the moment, as we have seen with ragtime, and here writing in response to a lingering demand for songs of the old 'drawing-room ballad' kind. This was popularised by the vivacious soubrette of the Metropolitan Opera, Fritzi Scheff (1879–1954), well known in Victor Herbert operettas.

I STOPPED, I LOOKED, AND I LISTENED. Music by Nat D. Ayer (1887–1952). Words by Clifford Grey (1887–1941). There were two shows of the First World War that all the troops on leave wanted to get back to see, 'The Bing Boys Are Here' (1916) and 'Chu Chin Chow' (1916). The first, really a glorified revue, had music written by Nat D. Ayer, an American entertainer who came to London with the American Ragtime Octet and stayed to write many successful stage shows (Clifford Grey was his most regular collaborator). 'The Bing Boys' starred George Robey, Alfred Lester and Violet Loraine and the writers cleverly wrote music to suit its stars. *If you were the only girl in the world**, *Another little drink* and this song which brings the art of George Robey to life every time we hear it.

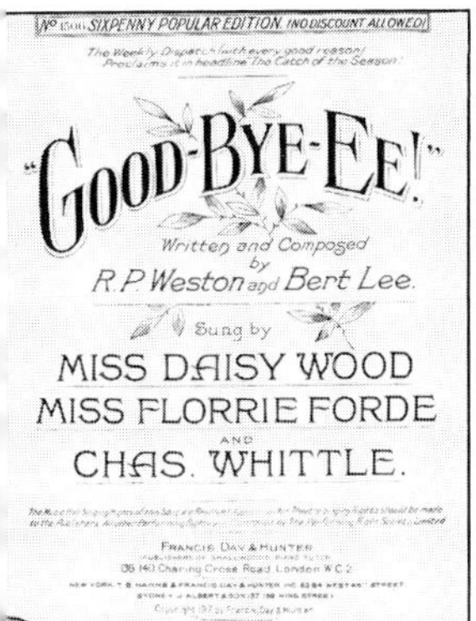

GOOD-BYE-EE. Music and words by R. P. Weston and Bert Lee. Still in the heat of World War I, published in 1917, this song has always had a nicely satirical touch about it that was well brought out when it was used, with others of the ilk, in 'Oh, What a Lovely War', stage-show and film. The satire is partly on the futility of the war, now beginning to be understood, and on the upper-class 'brother Berties' and the automatically acquired 'lieutenant pips upon his shoulder bright and gay'. He sometimes barely had time to put them up before he was another of the war's irretrievable casualties. It is interesting to find that one of its first interpreters was that irresistibly funny man Harry Tate (1873–1940) who was killed in an air-raid in World War II. Recorded by Courtland and Jefferies (World Records SH130); 'Oh, What a Lovely War' (Decca PA27, (S) SPA27).

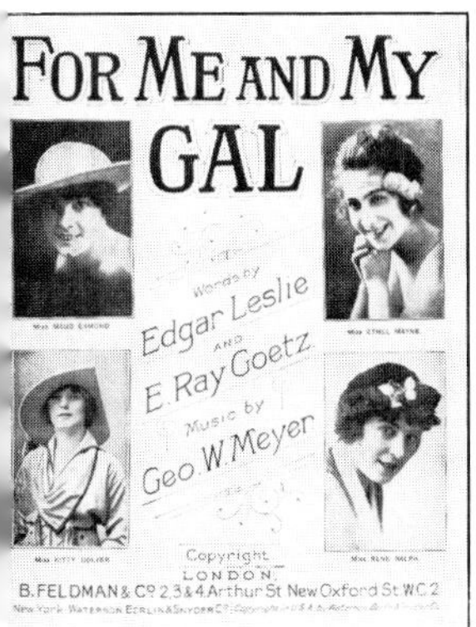

FOR ME AND MY GAL. Music by George W. Meyer (1884–1959). Words by Edgar Leslie (1885–1976) and Ray Goetz (1886–1954). This great song of 1917 was the best-seller of George Meyer, an amateur till 1909 when *Lonesome* became a hit, after which he kept up a regular flow of average songs and wrote for Broadway. With an ideal marriage of words and music, it was always a popular community favourite and had a new lease of life in 1943 when it was revived as the title song of a film starring Judy Garland and Gene Kelly.

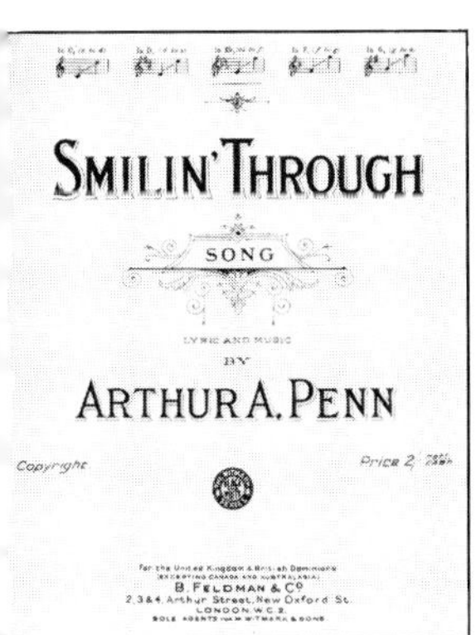

SMILIN' THROUGH. Music and words by Arthur A. Penn (1875–1941). Not to be confused with William H. Penn, Arthur A. was a London-born composer who went to America in 1903, started in publishing and founded his own business in 1906. He was a versatile writer in many fields. By a happy stroke of fate *Smilin' through*, published in 1918, was incorporated in a play then being written to star Jane Cowl; in fact, the play was rewritten at this stage to take in the song and used the same title. It made both a tremendous success. Later the song played the same incidental role in two film adaptations, a silent with Norma Talmadge and a talkie with Norma Shearer. The composer was able to buy a cottage (called 'Smilin' Through', of course) on the proceeds. Recorded by Jane Fyffe (Guilor (S) KS1006); John McCormack (Music for Pleasure MFP1090).

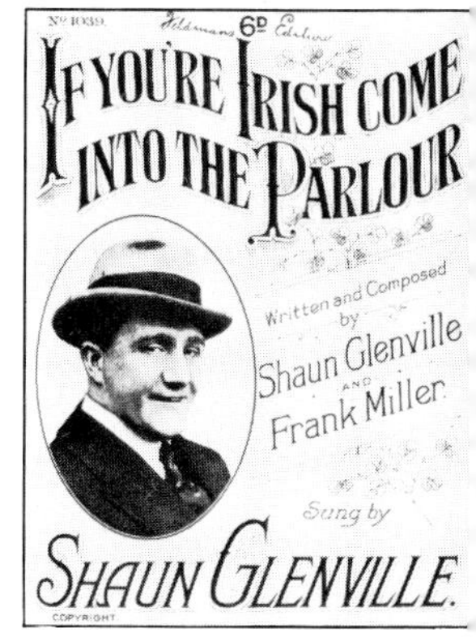

IF YOU'RE IRISH COME INTO THE PARLOUR. Music and words by Shaun Glenville and Frank Miller. One of the songs made famous by the Irish comedian and pantomime dame Shaun Glenville (1884–1968), who made his first music-hall appearance in England in 1906 and his London début at the Holborn Empire the following year. His line in Irish comedy songs included this one and *Something in the Irish After All, Mickey Rooney's Ragtime Band* and *He's a Credit to Old Ireland.* Successful in many kinds of popular entertainment, he became best-known for his pantomime dames, usually appearing with his wife Dorothy Ward as the equally famous principal boy.

I'M FOREVER BLOWING BUBBLES. Music and words by Jaan Kenbrovin and John William Kellette. This particular bit of idealistic philosophy, written in 1919 in the aftermath of War was the work of three writers, James Kendis (1883–1946), James Brockman (1886–1976) and Nat Vincent (1889–1979) who chose (whether in modesty or shame, we don't know) to hide their identities under the name of Jaan Kenbrovin. John W. Kellette, who composed the tune, was an actor. Born of the American vaudeville circuit, this is a song which easily manages to sound British by virtue of its old-fashioned sweetness and grace.

I BELONG TO GLASGOW. Music and words by Will Fyffe (1885–1947). Born in Dundee, Will Fyffe was soon in the entertainment business joining the family touring company. He persevered, without success, as a straight actor, began writing comedy material and eventually tried his hand in the provincial music halls. It was partly the bibulous song *I belong to Glasgow* which he wrote in 1921 and first sang at the Theatre Royal in Glasgow (after offering it to Harry Lauder and Neil Kenyon who were not interested) that led to his big chance. On the strength of it an agent signed him for the London Palladium and negotiated a contract for him to appear at the Glasgow Pavilion for the next three years. He was an excellent actor, a good singer and a fine mimic. All he needed was the one good song to lead him to the top of the variety tree. Recorded by Will Fyffe (World Records SH200).

THREE O'CLOCK IN THE MORNING. Music by Julian Robledo (1887–1940). Words by Dorothy Terriss (Theodora Morse) (1890–1953). Written in the strong tradition of the sweeping waltz song, and based

on the composer's piano piece published in New Orleans in 1919, London and Berlin 1920, it takes as its middle strain the famous chimes of Big Ben. With lyrics added it appeared in 'Greenwich Village Follies of 1921'. Judy Garland revived it in the film 'Presenting Lily Mars' in 1943 and it was also used in 'That Midnight Kiss' (1949). Paul Whiteman made a big-selling record, since when it has maintained a universal appeal.

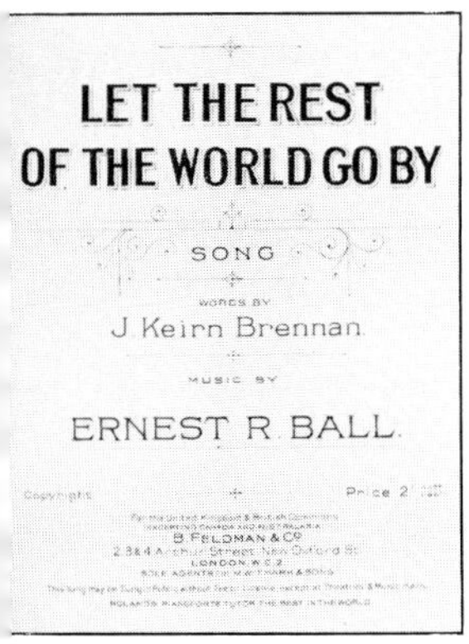

LET THE REST OF THE WORLD GO BY. Music by Ernest R. Ball (1878–1927). Words by J. Keirn Brennan (1873–1948). Ernest R. Ball was another famous American composer who was staff composer at the well-known House of Witmark. He was with them from 1907 to 1927 during which time he penned a very profitable list of best-sellers that included those sham-Irish public house favourites *Mother Machree* and *When Irish eyes are smiling* as well as that model of sentimental songs *Will you love me in December*. In 1919 he wrote *Let the rest of the world go by* and it appeared to be a great flop. Yet composer and publishers throught it had quality and resisted the temptation to drop it from their lists. Suddenly, for no specific reason, it began to catch on and by the outbreak of World War II had sold some $3\frac{1}{2}$ million copies. Recorded by Joan Morris (Nonesuch (S) H.71330); Frank Barber Shop Quartet (Music for Pleasure (S) MFP1375).

DON'T HAVE ANY MORE, MISSUS MOORE. Music and words by Harry Castling and James Walsh. As with the above song this one, written in 1926, shows evidence of an old tradition adapted for 20th-century humour, but it has lines which would have done service in the old halls like 'if you have any more, Missus Moore, you'll have to rent the house next door'. It was sung by Lily Morris (1884–1952) who was well known as a big-voiced singer of chorus songs in the Forde/Victoria tradition. *Why am I always the bridesmaid* was another of her hits. She appeared in the Royal Variety Performance of 1927, retired, then came back with the 'Thanks for the Memory' tour in 1948. Recorded by Lily Morris (World Records SH149).

EVERY LITTLE MOVEMENT HAS A MEANING OF ITS OWN. Music and words by Moore. A song surely written very much with Marie Lloyd in mind. One can imagine the sauciness of her performance and the actual movements which accompanied the words which have a strangely 'upper-crust' ring about them with their 'Johnnies' and 'Reggies'. It should not be confused, as it sometimes is, with the very lovely song which the American composer Karl Hoschna wrote for his 1910 musical comedy 'Madame Sherry'. Such a catchline as 'every little movement has a meaning of its own' was meat and drink to Marie Lloyd but the owners of the American copyright were not keen to have their fine song down-graded in the halls. So, as titles are not copyright, the new (and admittedly inferior) song was purpose written the following year. Recorded by Marie Lloyd (World Record Club SHB43; Rhapsody RHA6002).

ON MOTHER KELLY'S DOORSTEP. Music and words by George A. Stevens. This was a late entry to the music-hall song ranks but it was written in a fine tuneful vein that would have done service during any of the half-century preceding 1925. One notes a tendency toward a slightly more sickly sort of sentiment (perhaps creeping in from growing Hollywood influence) which dates it, along with the word 'kiddie' as of the 1920s. It became very much the song of Randolph Sutton (1888–1969) one of the last of the golden age stars who made his début at the London Pavilion in 1925 and made his last record in January 1969, a month before he died. It included *Mother Kelly*, of course. Since then others like Danny La Rue have made much of the song. Recorded by Randolph Sutton (Decca ACL1266).

RIDING ON TOP OF THE CAR. Music by Harry Von Tilzer. Words by Fred W. Leigh (d. 1924) and Alfred Bryan (1871–1958). An adaptation of an American song. It has a nice touch of humour. As we live in town, says the singer, we have no such things as lovers' lanes and rustic stiles so we have to do our courting on top of a tramcar – which we find very suitable for the purpose. It was sung by George Lashwood (1863–1942), one of the last of the lion-comiques, who had great hits with *Goodbye, Dolly Gray** and *In the twi-twi-twilight†*. The present song dates from 1904. Recorded by George Lashwood (World Record Club SHB22).

ARE WE TO PART LIKE THIS BILL? Music and words by Harry Castling and Charles Collins. One of the best sentimental songs of the later music hall, written in 1911 and 'immortalised by' Kate Carney (1870–1950), once described by James Agate as 'the last of the great *lionness comiques*'. She was a great portrayer of the girl with a broken heart or the orphaned child and would switch from broad humour to deep pathos. *Are we to part like this Bill* was her best number and there was never a dry eye in the house after her poignant but full-blooded rendering of 'Who's it ter be – 'er or me, don't be afraid to say!' Recorded by Kate Carney (Decca ACL1170); Ann Windsor (Saga (S) SOC1042).

WHAT DID SHE KNOW ABOUT RAILWAYS. Music by Bennett Scott. Words by C. G. Cotes. A song which combines two of the Marie Lloyd stocks-in-trade – the railway song, most famously represented by *Oh, Mr. Porter*; and the 'song of innocence', portraying the young girl, fresh from the country and her mother's care, who was perhaps not quite so innocent as she seemed. It is not difficult to imagine the innuendo which Marie Lloyd put into the seemingly simple chorus lines 'someone wanted to punch her ticket' – to which she replied 'she'd never had her ticket punched before'. What it lacks in distinction as a melody it makes up for in the naughty spirit that led respectable middle-class families of the time to forbid their daughters to visit the music-hall.

I'M JUST WILD ABOUT HARRY. Music and words by Noble Sissle (1889–1975) and Eubie Blake (1883–). Hearing Leslie Stuart's 'Florodora' inspired the black ragtime composer Eubie Blake to write for the theatre. In 1907 he was assistant conductor with the Jim Europe Band (the 369th Infantry Band during the War) and Blake took it over when Europe died in 1919. In 1915 he had joined forces with the bandleader Noble Sissle in a double vaudeville act and as a songwriting team. In 1921 they produced the first really successful black revue on Broadway, 'Shuffle Along', its biggest hit the song *I'm just wild about Harry.* A revival of interest in ragtime brought Blake out of retirement in his eighties to lecture, perform, record and broadcast and run his own record company.

DOWN AT THE OLD BULL AND BUSH. Music by Harry von Tilzer (1872–1946). Words by Andrew B. Sterling, Russell Hunting and Percy Krone. The compulsory ending to almost any 'Good Old Days' entertainment and the habitual finale at Leeds. Of American origin it got its very English character in a roundabout way. Florrie Forde, on tour in America, heard a Harry von Tilzer song that was being made into a great hit in 1902 by Nora Bayes – *Down where the Wurzburger flows.* Nora Bayes became known as the 'Wurzburger girl'; and Florrie Forde brought the song back to England. She was criticised in *The Times* for singing about foreign rivers: 'The Rhine may be fine but a cold stein for mine, down where the Wurzburger flows'. So she had the next Von Tilzer hit, an equally beery number called *Under the Anheuser Bush* (1903), adapted to the now familiar form of *Down at the Old Bull and Bush* – with the great success that followed. Recorded by Florrie Forde (Music for Pleasure MFP1146) (Decca ACL1170) (World Records SH145); Stanley Holloway (World Records (S) ST912).

* available in *Music Hall Song Book* (EMI Publishing/David & Charles)
† available in *60 Old-Time Variety Songs* (EMI Publishing)